Baden-Württemberg

SO SCHÖN IST UNSER LAND

Baden-Württemberg

Von Reinhard Pietsch

Englisch von Jane Michael

KNESEBECK

Inhalt
Contents

Seite 1: Der „Honigschlecker" in der Klosterkirche Birnau, Seite 2: Alt-stadt von Schwäbisch Hall. Seiten 3–4: Hohenzollernschloss Sigmaringen.

Page 1: The "Honigschlecker", Birnau. Page 2: The historic town center of Schwäbisch Hall. Page 3-4: The Hohenzollern Castle at Sigmaringen.

Baden-Württemberg – vom Südweststaat wider Willen ...

Baden-Württemberg – from reluctant southwest state ...

Baden-Württemberg ist als Folge des Zweiten Weltkriegs eigentlich ein Kunstgebilde. Das vereinte Bundesland erscheint uns heute längst natürlich und selbstverständlich, doch in weiten Teilen Badens war man anfangs vehement gegen diese Fusion. Das Grundgesetz sah 1949 eine Neuordnung der Länder vor – per Volksentscheid. Für die Abstimmung wurde das Gebiet des heutigen Bundeslands in vier Zonen eingeteilt – Nordwürttemberg, Südwürttemberg-Hohenzollern, Nord- und Südbaden. Das Abstimmungsverhalten war bekannt, die Württemberger waren mit über 90 Prozent für die Fusion; Nordbaden war mit 57 Prozent dabei. Südbaden lehnte den Zusammenschluss jedoch mehrheitlich ab: Nur 38 Prozent stimmten mit Ja. Der geschickte Zuschnitt der Abstimmungsbezirke stellte jedoch sicher, dass die erforderliche 3/4-Mehrheit zustande kam – der Südweststaat konnte 1952 gegründet werden. Vor dem Verfassungsgericht bekamen die Gegner zwar Recht. Doch Jahre später, bei dem zweiten Volksentscheid waren auch die Südbadener überzeugt: Im Juni 1970 stimmten fast 82 Prozent für das neue Bundesland.

Baden-Württemberg is actually an artificial structure formed in the aftermath of World War II. We have long since got used to the unified state, but in fact large sections of Baden were originally strongly against the amalgamation. In 1949 the Constitution of the Federal Republic provided for a redrawing of the boundaries between the Länder – by plebiscite. The region which makes up the state today was divided into four zones for the purpose of the vote. The way the different regions would vote was clear in advance: over 90 percent of the citizens of Württemberg and 57 percent of the inhabitants of North Baden were in favor of the fusion. Most of those living in South Baden were against it. Nonetheless, the skillful division of the voting regions ensured that the requisite three-quarters majority was attained: and the new state in Germany's southwest was founded in 1952. The residents of South Baden won their case when they appealed to the Constitutional Court. However, a second plebiscite only took place several years later: Having recognised the advantages by the time almost 82 percent voted in favor of the new state in June 1970.

Viele Städte in Baden-Württemberg haben einen gepflegten historischen Kern mit schönen, gut erhaltenen Fachwerkhäusern – wie hier in Schorndorf.

Many towns in Baden-Württemberg have an immaculate historic center with fine, timbered houses in excellent condition – as here in Schorndorf.

Eine Klischeevorstellung sieht den Badener als leichtfüßigen Genussmenschen, während der Schwabe eher wortkarg, sparsam, stur und fleißig sei. Das Bild ist überzogen, doch es enthält einen Kern von Wahrheit, der historisch begründet ist. Einen Schlüssel liefert das traditionelle Erbrecht: Während in den meisten württembergischen Gebieten der bäuerliche Grund in Realteilung auf alle Erbberechtigten verteilt und so immer kleiner wurde, galt in Baden das Anerbenrecht, der Hof fiel also an den jeweils ältesten Nachkommen. Die Württemberger Bauern mussten so immer kleinere Parzellen bewirtschaften. Fleiß, Sparsamkeit und harte Arbeit waren nötig, um zu überleben. In Baden hingegen hatte der Hoferbe noch ein gutes Auskommen; nachrangige Kinder wurden kaum abgefunden und mussten sich umsehen. Dem „leichtfüßigen" Badener blieb oft nichts anderes übrig, als auszuwandern. Not machte in Württemberg hingegen erfinderisch: Kein Wunder, dass hier auch die Industrie aufblühte und auf viele Arbeitskräfte zählen konnte, die von der Landwirtschaft nicht mehr leben konnten.

A popular cliché illustrates the native of Baden as a carefree bon-vivant, while the Swabian tends to be taciturn, thrifty, obstinate and hard-working. The Image is exaggerated, but it contains an element of truth which is rooted in historical fact. The key can be found to some extent in the traditional laws of inheritance: while most regions of Württemberg were subject to the division of property — which meant that the farmland was divided among all the heirs and thus became progressively smaller — in Baden the law of inheritance applied whereby the farm was left to the eldest son. The farmers in Württemberg thus had to earn their living from ever-smaller plots of land. Hard work and thriftiness were essential in order to survive. In Baden, by contrast, the heir who inherited the farm had a good income; younger children inherited very little and had to fend for themselves. The "light-footed" citizen of Baden often had no choice but to emigrate. In Württemberg, by contrast, necessity proved to be the mother of invention: it is not surprising that industry blossomed here and benefited from the large numbers of workers who could no longer make a living from the land.

Alt und neu in Stuttgart-Mitte – das Landtagsgebäude wurde zwischen 1959 und 1961 erbaut; in der Glasfront spiegelt sich das barocke Neue Schloss aus der zweiten Hälfte des 18. Jahrhunderts.

Old and new in the center of Stuttgart – the state parliament building was built between 1959 and 1961. Reflected in the glass façade is the Baroque Neues Schloss dating from the second half of the eighteenth century.

… zum stolzen „*Musterländle*"

… to model region

Vielleicht hat die „Zwangsehe" den Beteiligten inzwischen auch ganz gutgetan. Baden-Württemberg ist mit 35 752 Quadratkilometern und etwa 11 Millionen Einwohnern das drittgrößte Bundesland Deutschlands. Innerhalb Deutschlands und Europas zählt es zu den wirtschaftlich stärksten Regionen. Neben den großen Autoherstellern gibt es zahlreiche bedeutende mittelständische, oft familiengeführte Unternehmen, die nicht selten mit ihren Produkten sogar Weltmarktführer sind. Zugleich zählt Baden-Württemberg neben Mecklenburg-Vorpommern und Bayern zu den Haupturlaubszielen innerhalb Deutschlands. Schwerpunkte bilden hier der Schwarzwald und das Bodenseegebiet. An der Kultur wird nicht gespart. Baden-Württemberg verfügt über mehrere erstklassige Opern- und Schauspielhäuser, besonders herausragend ist dabei das Vierspartenhaus des Staatstheaters Stuttgart. Die Stuttgarter Oper wurde mehrfach zur „Oper des Jahres" gekürt, und das Ballett, an dem einst John Cranko und Marcia Haydée gewirkt haben, gilt noch immer als eines der besten der Welt. Doch auch die Traditionen werden mit großer Leidenschaft gepflegt, nicht zuletzt das Narrentreiben der farbenfrohen schwäbisch-alemannischen Fasnet. Die Baden-Württemberger sind stolz auf ihr Land. Der offizielle Werbeslogan klingt daher sehr selbstbewusst: „Wir können alles. Außer Hochdeutsch."

Perhaps this "shotgun marriage" between the two parties has proved beneficial in the long run. Baden-Württemberg covers an area of 35,752 square kilometers (13,804 square miles) and with about 11 million inhabitants it is the third-largest state in Germany. Economically speaking it is one of the strongest regions within Germany and even Europe. Apart from the major car makers there are countless important medium-sized companies, often family-owned, which are frequently world leaders in their branch. At the same time Baden-Württemberg is one of the top holiday regions in Germany, alongside Mecklenburg-West Pomerania and Bavaria. The highlights here include the Black Forest and Lake Constance. There is generous support for culture throughout the region. Baden-Württemberg has a number of first-class opera houses and theaters; the four-discipline Stuttgart State Theater is outstanding in this respect. The Stuttgart Opera has been elected "Opera Company of the Year" on several occasions, and the ballet, where once John Cranko and Marcia Haydée worked, is still considered to be one of the finest in the world. Traditions are maintained with great enthusiasm, too, especially the carnival antics of the Swabian-Alemannic Fasnet. The citizens of Baden-Württemberg are proud of their homeland. Even their slogan sounds self-confident: "We can do everything. Except speak High German."

Weinbau hat in Baden-Württemberg eine lange Tradition – im Bild das Tal bei Oberkirch im Ortenaukreis, nördlicher Schwarzwald.

Wine has been cultivated in Baden-Württemberg for centuries; the photo shows the valley near Oberkirch in the Ortenau district in the northern Black Forest.

Stuttgart und Umgebung – Kernland Schwabens

Stuttgart and surroundings – the Swabian heartland

Die Landeshauptstadt von Baden-Württemberg hat viel zu bieten – und mit ihr das Umland. Hier sind die Schwaben zu Hause, hier gilt das Motto „Schaffen, sparen, Häusle bauen" bis heute. An Schlössern, historischen Kirchen und gepflegten mittelalterlichen Altstädten herrscht kein Mangel. Industrie und Mittelstand – mit Schwerpunkten im Maschinenbau und in der Automobilindustrie – zeigen aber auch, dass die Region alles andere als verschlafen ist.

The capital of Baden-Württemberg has a great deal to offer – and with it the surrounding region. This is the homeland of the Swabians, whose motto remains to this day "Work, save, build a house." There is no shortage of castles, historic churches and well cared-for historic city centers. Industry and medium-sized firms – especially mechanical engineering and the automobile industry – also prove that the region is certainly wide awake.

Stuttgart – Stadt der Parks und Weinberge

Stuttgart – the city of parks and vineyards

Mit Stuttgart werden international vor allem zwei Autohersteller in Verbindung gebracht – Mercedes-Benz und Porsche. Sogar der Bahnhof grüßt mit dem bekannten Stern. Doch wirkt die schwäbische Metropole überhaupt nicht wie eine typische Industrie- und Autostadt. Im Gegenteil: Keine rauchenden Schlote, sondern Parks und Grünanlagen prägen ihr Erscheinungsbild. Die Innenstadt liegt in einem Kessel und ist umgeben von Weinbergen und Wäldern. Auffallend sind die mehr als 400 Treppen („Stäffele"), die meist auf ehemalige Weinbergstaffeln zurückgehen, und tiefer gelegene mit höher gelegenen Wohngebieten verbinden. Stuttgart wurde im Zweiten Weltkrieg fast völlig zerstört. Von der alten Substanz konnte jedoch manches wieder gerettet und restauriert werden: Dazu gehören der Schillerplatz mit dem Alten Schloss, einem imposanten Renaissancebau, und das barocke Neue Schloss. Die beiden Schlösser und einige andere Sehenswürdigkeiten reihen sich entlang der Königsstraße, der zentralen Achse vom Rotebühlplatz bis zum Hauptbahnhof – heute Fußgängerzone mit zahlreichen Geschäften. Am Südrand des Kessels, auf der 200 Meter höheren Filderebene im Stadtteil Degerloch erhebt sich der knapp 217 Meter hohe, 1956 eingeweihte Fernsehturm – weltweit der erste Sendeturm aus Stahlspannbeton. Von der Aussichtsplattform in 150 Metern Höhe hat man eine herrlichen Aussicht.

The names of two international automobile manufacturers are automatically associated with Stuttgart: Mercedes Benz and Porsche. Even the railroad station greets visitors with the famous star on its roof. And yet, the Swabian metropolis does not look in the least like a typical industrial and automobile city. On the contrary: there are no smoking factory chimneys, but rather the city is characterized by its parks and open spaces. The city center lies in a basin surrounded by vineyards and forests. Typical are the more than 400 stairs known as "Stäffele", which mostly hark back to former vineyard terraces and which link lower and higher residential areas. Stuttgart was almost completely destroyed during World War II. Some of the old buildings were restored: they include Schillerplatz with the Old Castle, an imposing Renaissance building, and the Baroque New Castle. The two castles and a number of other sights are lined up along Königsstrasse, the central axis leading from Rotebühlplatz to the main station – today a pedestrian street lined with shops. On the southern edge of the basin, on the Filderebene (200 m/ 656 ft) in the Degerloch district, stands the television tower (217 m/ 712 ft) which was dedicated in 1956: the first transmission tower in the world to be built of prestressed reinforced concrete. From the observation platform at a height of 150 meters (492 feet) there is a magnificent view of the city.

Seite 12, 13 von links im Uhrzeigersinn: Neues Schloss, Stuttgart. Schloss Favorite in Ludwigsburg. Literaturmuseum der Moderne, Marbach am Neckar. Marktplatz und Palmsche Apotheke, Schorndorf. Esslingen, Burg.

Page 12,13, clockwise from the left: Neues Schloss, Stuttgart. Favorite palace in Ludwigsburg. The Museum of Modern Literature in Marbach am Neckar. Market place and Palmsche Apotheke, Schorndorf. Esslingen Castle.

Von links oben im Uhrzeigersinn: Neue Staatsgalerie, Altes Schloss mit Reiterfigur, Schloss Solitude, Volksfest Cannstatter Wasen.

Clockwise from top left: Neue Staatsgalerie. Altes Schloss with equestrian statue. Schloss Solitude. The Cannstatter Wasen folk festival.

Die schönsten Museen – Kunst und Technik

The finest museums – art and technology

Über 40 Museen hat Stuttgart vorzuweisen. Ein Spitzenplatz unter den europäischen Kunstmuseen gebührt dabei der Staatsgalerie, die über einen alten und einen neuen Teil verfügt. Während im klassizistischen Altbau Kunstwerke vom Mittelalter bis zum 19. Jahrhundert gezeigt werden, legt der von James Stirling entworfene monumentale neue Gebäudekomplex den Schwerpunkt auf die Kunst des 20. Jahrhunderts und der Gegenwart. Dieser Erweiterungsbau wurde 1984 eingeweiht und zählt längst zu den architektonischen Wahrzeichen der Stadt. Wer die Königsstraße entlangschlendert, stößt am Kleinen Schlossplatz unweigerlich auf das 2005 eröffnete Kunstmuseum Stuttgart. Der gewaltige Kubus aus Glas enthält neben wechselnden Ausstellungen unter anderem die umfangreichste Sammlung von Werken des Malers Otto Dix (1891–1969), der für seine sozialkritischen Bilder im Stil der Neuen Sachlichkeit bekannt ist. Der „Kunstwürfel" ist besonders nachts ein spektakulärer Anblick, wenn durch die Beleuchtung die Travertinwände im Inneren sichtbar werden und die Glasfassaden mit wechselnden meterhohen Buchstaben- und Wortfolien beklebt sind.

Stuttgart can boast over 40 museums. The Staatsgalerie is one of the top art museums in Europe, consisting of an old and new section. In the neo-classical old building you can see masterpieces from the Middle Ages to the 19th century, while the monumental new complex designed by James Stirling focuses on twentieth-century and contemporary art. The extension was dedicated in 1984 and has long since been included among the town's architectural landmarks. After strolling down Königsstrasse to the Kleiner Schlossplatz you will inevitably arrive in front of the Kunstmuseum Stuttgart, opened in 2005. The massive glass cube contains – apart from changing exhibitions – a comprehensive collection of works by Otto Dix (1891-1969), who is famous for his socially critical paintings in the style of the New Objectivity. The cube-like art museum is particularly dramatic at night when the illumination makes the travertine inner walls visible from the outside and the glass façade is decorated with changing letters and words up to one meter high.

Faszination Technik – in Baden-Württemberg befindet sich die Wiege des Automobils: 1886 baute Carl Benz in Mannheim sein erstes dreirädriges Fahrzeug mit Verbrennungsmotor, wenig später folgte unabhängig davon Gottlieb Daimler in Cannstatt mit seiner Motorkutsche. Beide Namen stehen seither für eine der großen Automarken der Welt. Die Geschichte dieser Marke wird im 2006 neu eröffneten Mercedes-Benz-Museum eindrucksvoll in Szene gesetzt. Auf 17 000 m² Ausstellungsfläche verteilt über neun Etagen kann der Be-

sucher den ersten erhaltenen Mercedes-Simplex von 1902 – eine 40 PS starke Konstruktion von Wilhelm Maybach – ebenso bestaunen wie die rote, gepanzerte Staatskarosse, die 1935 für den japanischen Kaiser Hirohito angefertigt wurde und immerhin bereits 150 PS leistete. Von den legendären Silberpfeilen bis zum aktuellen McLaren-Mercedes sind viele Traumautos zu sehen. Auch die Sparte der Mercedes-Nutzfahrzeuge kommt nicht zu kurz – historische Omnibusse, Lkws, Polizei-, Kranken- und Feuerwehrautos. Ein tragbarer Audioguide liefert zu jedem Exponat detaillierte Informationen.

The fascination of technology can be seen in Baden-Württemberg, the cradle of the automobile. In 1886 Carl Benz built his first three-wheeled vehicle with an internal combustion engine; independently of Benz, Gottlieb Daimler followed shortly afterwards in Cannstatt. Since then both names have stood for one of the world's greatest automobile brands. The Mercedes-Benz Museum, opened in 2006, narrates impressively the story of the brand. Across an area of 17,000 sq.m (182,920 sq. ft) and nine floors the visitor can admire the first surviving Mercedes Simplex of 1902, a 40-horsepower construction by Wilhelm Maybach, as well as the red armored state car built in 1935 for Emperor Hirohito of Japan and which could produce 150 hp. There are countless dream automobiles to admire, from the legendary Silver Arrows to the latest McLaren-Mercedes. There is also a section devoted to Mercedes utility vehicles – historic omnibuses, trucks, police cars, ambulances and fire engines. A portable audio guide can be obtained at the cash desk and supplies detailed information about each of the exhibits.

Böblingen, Weil der Stadt, Waiblingen

Böblingen, Weil der Stadt, Waiblingen

Ähnlich wie Stuttgart ist auch die an einem steilen Ausläufer des Schönbuchs gelegene Innenstadt von Böblingen durch zahlreiche Treppen geprägt. Die Kreisstadt im Südwesten von Stuttgart bildet mit Sindelfingen – dort befindet sich das weltweit größte Automobilwerk der Daimler AG – ein Mittelzentrum für die umliegenden Gemeinden. Wahrzeichen ist die spätgotische, evangelische Stadtkirche aus dem 14. Jahrhundert. Zum Landkreis gehört Weil der Stadt, bekannt als Geburtsort von Johannes Kepler (1571–1630), der die nach ihm benannten Gesetze der Planetenbewegung entdeckte. Kepler gilt als einer der Begründer der modernen Naturwissenschaft, er selbst war jedoch zeitlebens mit gleicher Leidenschaft Mystiker und Astrologe. Sein Geburtshaus ist heute ein Museum. In der Altstadt von Weil der Stadt befinden sich zahlreiche mittelalterliche Handwerkerhäuser. Besonders sehenswert ist die spätgotische Stadtkirche St. Peter und Paul mit ihrem großen Barockaltar. Eine gut erhaltene Altstadt zeichnet auch die nordöstlich von Stuttgart gelegene Kreisstadt Waiblingen aus, die sich zu beiden Seiten der Rems erstreckt. Die Stauferstadt, die 1250 das Stadtrecht erhielt, liegt an der Deutschen Fachwerkstraße und der Württembergischen Weinstraße. Zahlreiche Fachwerkhäuser, darunter das Museum der Stadt Waiblingen und das alte Rathaus mit seinen Arkaden, bereichern das Stadtbild.

Like Stuttgart, the town center of Böblingen is characterized by countless steps thanks to its location on a steep ridge of the Schönbuch. Together with Sindelfingen, the largest automobile factory of Daimler AG, the district town to the southwest of Stuttgart forms a focal point for the surrounding communities. The most prominent landmark is the late-Gothic parish church dating from the 14th century, now Protestant. Also lying within the district boundaries is Weil der Stadt, famous as the birthplace of Johannes Kepler (1571–1630), who discovered the Kepler Laws of planetary motion named after him. Kepler is regarded as one of the founders of modern science, but he himself remained all his life both a mystic and an astrologer. The house in which he was born is now a museum. In the old town you will find a large number of medieval craftsmen's houses. Of particular note is the late-Gothic parish church of St. Peter and St. Paul, which has a large Baroque altar. Waiblingen, a well-preserved district town northeast of Stuttgart, also boasts a well-preserved old town center; it lies on both banks of the River Rems. The town, formerly the property of the Hohenstaufens, was awarded municipal rights in 1250 and lies on the German Timbered Buildings Road and the Württemberg Wine Road. The town's appearance is enhanced by numerous timbered buildings, including the arcaded old Town Hall.

Altstadt von Waiblingen, im Hintergrund der Turm der historischen Nikolauskirche, die seit 1982 von der griechisch-orthodoxen Gemeinde genutzt wird.

The old town of Waiblingen. In the background can be seen the tower of the historic Church of St. Nicholas, which has been used by the Greek Orthodox community since 1982.

SPECIAL | Spargel, Spätzle und Maultaschen

Asparagus, Spätzle and Maultaschen

Rustikal – die Küche Württembergs

Teigwaren spielen in dieser bodenständigen Küche ein große Rolle, zu allererst die Spätzle, die nur wirklich „echt" sind, wenn der ausgerollte Teig direkt vom Brett ins kochende Wasser „geschabt" wird. Das klassische Gericht, das im Herbst sehr beliebt ist und dann in vielen schwäbischen Gastwirtschaften auf der Karte steht, ist die Kombination mit Linsen und Saiten, eine Art Frankfurter Würstchen; gut dazu passt etwas durchwachsener gebratener Speck. Ein weiteres typisches Nudelgericht sind die Käs'spätzle, ein nahrhafter Auflauf, bei dem die Teigwaren mit Käse, meist Emmentaler, überbacken und mit gerösteten Zwiebeln bestreut serviert werden. Nicht zu vergessen sind auch die Maultaschen, die entweder in der Brühe, oder „geschmälzt", also mit in Butter braun gebratenen Zwiebeln, auf den Tisch kommen. Das klassische Sonntagsgericht ist der Zwiebelrostbraten. Als Fleisch wird hier Roastbeef verwendet, als Beilage werden in Schwaben Spätzle gereicht, mit reichlich Soße. Und dazu darf es dann auch ein „Viertele", ein Glas Wein sein – natürlich ein Trollinger.

Rustic – the cuisine of Württemberg

Pasta plays an important role in the down-to-earth cuisine of Württemberg. Spätzle, the local home-made noodles, are only genuine when the dough is scraped directly from the board into the boiling water. The classic dish, which is very popular in fall and which is then found on the menu of countless Swabian inns, is the combination with lentils and Saiten, a type of sausage rather like a frankfurter; it tastes particularly good with fried streaky bacon. Another typical pasta dish is Käs'spätzle, a hearty baked noodle dish in which the pasta is mixed with cheese, usually Emmental, before being gratinated and sprinkled with dry-fried onions. Nor should we forget the Maultaschen, a sort of local ravioli which are either served in broth or with onions fried in butter. The classic Sunday roast is Zwiebelrostbraten, which is also very popular in Austria. It is made using beef and is served with Spätzle. With a "Viertele", a glass of wine – a Trollinger, of course.

Maultaschen sind eine schwäbische Spezialität. Die Teigtaschen werden mit einer Mischung aus Brät, Spinat und Zwiebeln gefüllt.

Maultaschen are a Swabian specialty. They are pockets of pasta filled with a mixture of meat, spinach and onions.

Französisch beeinflusst – die Küche Badens

Die westlichen Nachbarn haben in Baden auch kulinarisch ihre Spuren hinterlassen – die Küche gilt als eine der besten in ganz Deutschland. Das liegt nicht nur an den beiden Dreisterneköchen in Baiersbronn, sondern ist tief in der Tradition verankert. Da hier verschiedene Einflüsse aufeinander treffen, ist es schwierig, ein ganz typisches Gericht zu benennen. Vielleicht ist es der Spargelteller in der klassischen Form mit feiner Butter oder Sauce hollandaise und neuen Kartoffeln oder auch kombiniert mit Flädle oder Kratzete aus Pfannkuchenteig. Europas größter Spargelmarkt findet in Nordbaden, in Bruchsal, statt. Über das Elsass lernte man die leckeren, mit Kräuterbutter überbackenen Weinbergschnecken kennen und das „Choucroute", feines Sauerkraut mit Fleisch und Wurst kombiniert. Am Bodensee versteht man es, den dort gefangenen Fisch raffiniert zuzubereiten, darunter den Egli. Überhaupt kommt viel Frisches auf den Tisch. Dazu wird ein passender Weißwein gereicht – mal ein kräftiger Ruländer, ein leichter Silvaner oder ein spritziger Weißherbst.

French influence – the cuisine of Baden

Baden's neighbor to the west has left its traces in the cuisine of the region: the cuisine is considered to be one of the best in the whole of Germany. That is not just because of the two three-star chefs in Baiersbronn; it is also deeply anchored in local tradition. Since various influences meet and are at work here, it is difficult to name a typical dish. Maybe it is a plate of asparagus, served classically with melted butter or sauce hollandaise and new potatoes or combined with Flädle or Kratzete made of pancake batter. The largest market for asparagus in Europe is held in Bruchsal in north Baden. From Alsace the locals learned to prepare the delicious snails baked with herb butter as well as "choucroute", fine sauerkraut combined with meat and sausages. On the shores of Lake Constance the freshly-caught local fish, such as perch, are prepared in sophisticated ways. Fresh ingredients predominate in the kitchen. Depending on the dish, a white wine is served – either a powerful Ruländer, a light Silvaner or a spirited Weissherbst.

Der schwäbische Klassiker: Linsen mit Spätzle und Saiten, so nennt man hier die Frankfurter Würstchen, lassen Schwabenherzen höherschlagen.

The classic Swabian dish: lentils with spätzle, a sort of pasta, and saiten – the local name for frankfurters. It is sure to delight any true native of the region.

Barockes Ludwigsburg und Umland

Baroque Ludwigsburg and surroundings

Der französische Absolutismus war für die Fürsten Württembergs nicht nur politisches, sondern auch ästhetisches Modell: Das barocke Residenzschloss (1704–1733) in Ludwigsburg wurde an Versailles angelehnt, die streng gegliederte Parkanlage, bekannt als „Blühendes Barock", erinnert ebenfalls an das französische Vorbild. Das Schloss verfügt über 452 Räume, auf einer eineinhalbstündigen Führung bekommt man etwa 65 davon zu sehen. Dieser Parcours ist zugleich eine Zeitreise in die Vergangenheit von den Stilepochen des Empire über Rokoko zum Barock. Im Park gegenüber der Nordfront befindet sich das kleinere Schlösschen Favorite. Teile der Parkanlage sind übrigens als „Märchengarten" gestaltet, in dem Kinder neben etwa 30 anderen Märchenszenen die Knusperhexe aus „Hänsel und Gretel" hervorlocken oder den Wolf bei den sieben Geißlein mimen können. In der Umgebung von Ludwigsburg lohnt ein Abstecher nach Bietigheim-Bissingen mit dem Unteren Tor, einem schönen Fachwerkbau, und dem großartigen Eisenbahnviadukt (Mitte 19. Jahrhundert), dem Wahrzeichen der Stadt. Wer einen Spaziergang durch ein mittelalterliches Städtchen machen möchte, dem sei der Luftkurort Besigheim am Zusammenfluss von Neckar und Enz ans Herz gelegt. Auf den Spuren Friedrich Schillers wandelt man hingegen im schönen Marbach, dem Geburtsort des Dichters.

French absolutism served as a political and esthetic model for the princes of Württemberg: the Baroque palace which was their residence (1704-1733) was modeled on Versailles; the geometrically designed park, often described as "Blossoming Baroque", also recalls the French model. The castle contains 452 rooms; the guided tour, which lasts about 1 1/2 hours, covers some 65 of them. The circuit is like a journey into the past, via the Empire and Rococo periods back to the Baroque.
In the park facing the north front lies little Favorite palace. Part of the park is laid out as a "Märchengarten" ("Fairy-Tale Garden"), in which children can press a button which brings out the witch in "Hansel and Gretel" or imitate the wolf and the seven little kids, as well as viewing about 30 other fairy-tale scenes. Near Ludwigsburg it is worth making a detour to Bietigheim-Bissingen to see the Unteres Tor, an attractive timbered building, and especially the magnificent railroad viaduct (mid-nineteenth century), the town's most prominent landmark. If you enjoy leisurely walks through a medieval town, you should visit the health resort of Besigheim at the confluence of the Neckar and the Enz. In lovely Marbach you can retrace the steps of the poet Friedrich Schiller, who was born there.

Barockschloss Ludwigsburg. Eisenbahnviadukt in Bietigheim-Bissingen. Altstadt von Besigheim. Oberer Torturm mit Stadtwappen von Marbach am Neckar.

Baroque Ludwigsburg palace. The railroad viaduct at Bietigheim-Bissingen. The historic town center of Besigheim. The Oberer Torturm tower with the coat of arms of Marbach am Neckar.

Esslingen, Schorndorf, Kirchheim unter Teck

Esslingen, Schorndorf, Kirchheim unter Teck

Esslingen am Neckar, Luftbild. Burg Teck bei Kirchheim unter Teck.

Esslingen on the Neckar, aerial view. Teck Castle near Kirchheim unter Teck.

In der Stauferstadt Esslingen lohnt ein Besuch der evangelischen Stadtkirche St. Dionysius mit ihren fünf, überraschend gut erhaltenen Glasfenstern aus dem 13. Jahrhundert. Auffallend ist auch das spätgotische Rathaus mit seiner roten Renaissanceschaufront. Esslingen ist der Stammsitz der 1826 gegründeten Kessler Sekt GmbH, der ältesten Sektkellerei Deutschlands. In Schorndorf, einige Kilometer weiter östlich, kam der Autopionier Gottlieb Daimler zur Welt (1834–1900). Die Palm'sche Apotheke (1660) am historischen Marktplatz gilt als eines der schönsten Fachwerkhäuser Süddeutschlands. Das Wahrzeichen von Kirchheim unter Teck ist das Fachwerk-Rathaus mit seiner Mondphasenuhr.

In Esslingen the parish church of St. Dionysius is worth visiting for its five surprisingly well-preserved stained-glass windows (13th century). Also of note is the late-Gothic Town Hall with its red Renaissance decorative façade. Esslingen is the headquarters of Kessler Sekt, the oldest manufacturer of sparkling wine in Germany. Automobile pioneer Gottlieb Daimler (1834-1900) was born in Schorndorf, a few kilometers further east. The Palmsche Apotheke (1660) on the historic marketplace is considered one of the finest timbered buildings in south Germany. Kirchheim unter Teck's landmark is the Town Hall with its clock showing the phases of the moon.

Schwäbische Alb – Höhlen, Quellen und Fossile

Swabian Alb – caves, springs and fossils

Die raue Alb wird klimatisch ihrem Ruf durchaus gerecht. Die Winde wehen kräftiger und kälter als im Flachland, das Leben war dort schon immer härter und hat einen entsprechenden Menschenschlag hervorgebracht. Selbst das Schwäbisch, das in den Dörfern gesprochen wird, klingt rauer. Vor Urzeiten war hier ein Meer, Wanderer stoßen deshalb im Kalkstein immer wieder auf Versteinerungen. Von der ruhmreichen jüngeren Vergangenheit zeugen zahlreiche Burgen und Schlösser.

Climatically speaking, the bleak Alb lives up to its reputation. The wind here blows colder and stronger than in the lowlands. Life here was always harsher and the people correspondingly more resilient. Even the Swabian dialect spoken in the villages sounds harder. In prehistoric times there was a sea here, and the limestone rocks contain fossils. The numerous castles and palaces bear witness to a more recent, glorious past.

Ulm, ein Spatz und ein Schneider

Ulm, a sparrow and a tailor

Der Ulmer Spatz ist in der Donaustadt allgegenwärtig – viele Geschäfte schmücken sich mit dem Wahrzeichen, und auch am Münster ist ein Vogel zu sehen, der allerdings eher einer Taube als einem Spatz gleicht. Eigentlich erscheinen die Ulmer Handwerker in dieser Sage in keinem besonders vorteilhaftem Licht: Beim Bau des Münsters wussten sie offenbar nicht, wie sie einen großen Balken durch das zu schmale Stadttor tragen sollten, und waren schon fast soweit, das Tor einzureißen; ein Licht gingen ihnen auf, als sie einen Spatz bemerkten, der einen sperrigen Halm einfach längs durch eine kleine Öffnung schob. Auch der legendäre Schneider von Ulm, Albrecht Ludwig Berblinger (1770–1829), war zwar ein Pionier auf seinem Gebiet, zugleich aber auch eine eher traurige Gestalt – seine Fluggeräte, den Vögeln abgeschaut, wollten einfach nicht fliegen. Ungetrübten Weltruhm erlangte hingegen ein anderer Sohn der Stadt, Albert Einstein (1879–1955), der Begründer der Relativitätstheorie. „Hoch hinaus" scheint das Motto der Stadt zu sein, immerhin kann sie mit dem höchsten Kirchturm der Welt (161,5 Meter) aufwarten. Die Innenstadt wurde im Zweiten Weltkrieg weitgehend zerstört, der Wiederaufbau ist nicht überall besonders gut gelungen. Bewusst neue interessante Akzente wurden am Münsterplatz mit dem Stadthaus und der „gläsernen Pyramide" der neuen Stadtbibliothek gesetzt.

The Sparrow of Ulm can be seen everywhere in the cathedral town on the Danube: it adorns numerous shops, and there is even a bird on the cathedral, althought it actually looks more like a pigeon than a sparrow. The Ulm craftsmen in the ancient myth do not appear in a very favorable light: apparently, when they were building the cathedral, they did not know how to get a large wooden beam through the narrow town gateway. They were on the verge of demolishing the gateway, but then the light dawned as they watched a sparrow which simply pushed a long straw lengthways through a small opening. The legendary Tailor of Ulm, Albrecht Ludwig Berblinger (1770-1829), was a pioneer in his field, but at the same time rather a sad character: his flying machines, which he produced by watching birds, simply refused to work. The world fame of another local son, however, was not clouded in any way: Albert Einstein (1879-1955), the inventor of the Theory of Relativity. "The sky's the limit" would appear to be the town's motto: indeed, it can claim the highest church spire in the world (161.5 meters/ 529.7 feet). The town center was largely destroyed by bombing during World War II; the rebuilding was not always as successful as it might have been. Interesting modern accents are set by the Stadthaus on Cathedral Square and the "glass pyramid" of the new Town Library.

Seite 26, 27: Burg Hohenzollern bei Hechingen, Statuen der Hohenzollernherrscher entlang der Burgmauer. Das Hohenzollernschloss Sigmaringen. Astronomische Uhr am Rathaus Ulm. Fachwerkfassade in Schwäbisch Gmünd.

Seite 26, 27: Hohenzollern Castle near Hechingen. Statues of the Hohenzollern rulers on the castle wall. The Hohenzollern castle at Sigmaringen. Astronomical clock on Ulm Town Hall. Timbered façade in Schwäbisch Gmünd.

Marktplatz von Ulm mit Ulmer Münster, dessen Turm der höchste Kirchturm der Welt ist.

The market place in Ulm with Ulm Cathedral, which boasts the tallest church spire in the world.

Das Fischerviertel – Ulm wie aus dem Bilderbuch

The Fischerviertel – picture postcard Ulm

Ulm gilt heute als die „gesündeste Großstadt" Deutschlands – bietet also seinen Bürgern beste Lebensbedingungen. Die Donaustadt kann auf eine lange Geschichte zurückblicken. Bereits im frühen Mittelalter, etwa um 850, gab es hier eine Königspfalz, die auch der damalige König Ludwig der Deutsche häufig besuchte. Diese Pfalz war wohl die Keimzelle für den Ort, der als Markt seinen Anfang nahm. Nachdem die Pfalz in der Zeit der sächsischen Könige (10. und 11. Jahrhundert) an Bedeutung verloren hatte, wurde sie erst wieder unter den Staufern im 12. Jahrhundert zu einem der wichtigsten Stützpunkte – Reste der Befestigungsmauer sind heute noch im malerischen Fischerviertel zu sehen. Um 1500 erlebte die Stadt eine wirtschaftliche Blüte und wurde sprichwörtlich für ihren Reichtum. Das „Ulmer Geld" beruhte in dieser Zeit

auf dem Barchent, einem Mischgewebe aus Leinen und Baumwolle, das damals reines Leinen ablöste. Ulm war eine der Hochburgen des in ganz Europa begehrten Stoffs. Gegen Ende des 19. Jahrhunderts verlor diese Art der Weberei aber an Bedeutung.

Ulm is described today as the "healthiest large town" in Germany, because it offers its citizens the best living conditions. The town on the Danube can look back on a long history. Even in the Middle Ages, around 850, there was a royal residence here, in which King Ludwig the German often resided. The palace formed the nucleus around which the town grew up, starting as a market place. Under the reign of the Saxon kings (10th and 11th centuries) the palace ceased to be so important, but during the 12th century under the Hohenstaufen dynasty it once again became one of their principal bases: remains of the fortifications from this period can still be seen in the picturesque Fischerviertel today. In around 1500 the town enjoyed a period of economic prosperity and was a byword for its wealth. Ulm's fortune was based in those days on fustian, a material made from a mixture of linen and cotton which was replacing pure linen at the time. Ulm was one of the European centers for the production of the fabric. Towards the end of the nineteenth century, however, the weaving trade lost its importance here.

Das malerische Fischerviertel in Ulm, hier fließt die Blau in die Donau.

The picturesque Fischerviertel in Ulm at the confluence of the Blau and the Danube.

Bereits im Mittelalter besiedelten Handwerker die Gegend um den Donauzufluss der Blau, dem heutigen Fischer- und Gerberviertel. Dort sind besonders viele schöne historische Gebäude erhalten geblieben, darunter das Schwörhaus, in dem heute das Haus der Stadtgeschichte untergebracht ist. Im frühen Mittelalter stand an dieser Stelle die Königspfalz; zwischen dem 14. und dem 19. Jahrhundert war das Haus ein bedeutender Weinhandelsplatz. Vom Balkon dieses Hauses aus wird traditionell jedes Jahr im Juli am „Schwörmontag" der historische Eid auf die Stadtverfassung von 1397 zelebriert. An der Staufermauer an der Blau befindet sich das sogenannte Schiefe Haus, ein Gebäude, das seinem Namen alle Ehre macht. Heute beherbergt es ein modern ausgestattetes Hotel. Die Neigung der Räume beträgt zwar noch immer bis zu 40 Zentimeter, was den speziellen Reiz ausmacht. Die Betten stehen allerdings absolut waagerecht – als Beleg sind an den Kopfteilen Wasserwaagen angebracht. Ein weiteres schönes Gebäude befindet sich gegenüber: die Alte Münz. Bis 1624 diente sie als Münzstätte, danach bis etwa 1900 als Schleif- und Ölmühle – das Wasserrad an der Südseite weist auf diese Art der Nutzung.

During the Middle Ages craftsmen settled in the district around the confluence of the Danube and the Blau, in what is now the fishermen's and tanners' district. A large number of fine historic buildings have survived here, including the Schwörhaus, which now houses the House of Local History. During the early Middle Ages the royal palace stood on this site; and between the fourteenth and nineteenth centuries the house was an important wine-trading establishment. Every year in July the historic oath on the town constitution of 1397 is celebrated from the balcony on "Schwörmontag". On the Staufermauer alongside the Blau stands the so-called "Crooked House", a building which really lives up to its name. Today it houses a modern hotel. The rooms slope by up to 40 centimeters (16 inches), but the beds are absolutely horizontal: there are even spirit levels attached to the bedheads to prove the fact.

Opposite the hotel you will find another fine building, the Alte Münz, which served as the town mint until 1624. Afterwards, until about 1900, it was a grinding and oil mill; the water wheel on the south side proves that it was used in this way.

Im „Schiefen Haus" befindet sich heute ein komfortables Hotel.

Today the "Schiefes Haus" houses a comfortable hotel.

Blaubeuren und der Blautopf

Blaubeuren and the Blautopf

Die größte und tiefste Quelle Deutschlands befindet sich in Blaubeuren am Fuß der Schwäbischen Alb. Sie wird Blautopf genannt, ist 21 Meter tief und speist die Blau, einen Fluss, der nach etwa 15 Kilometern auf Ulmer Stadtgebiet in die Donau mündet. Geologisch gesehen handelt es sich um eine Karstquelle, also eine Quelle, die durch Wasser gespeist wird, das an anderer Stelle versickert ist. Die intensive blaue Farbe der Quelle beruht auf dem hohen Kalkgehalt des Wassers, die kurzwelligen blauen Anteile des Lichts werden deshalb stärker gestreut. 1985 wurde bei einem Tauchgang im Blautopf ein riesiges Höhlensystem mit Tropfsteinen entdeckt. Direkt an der Quelle befindet sich die sehenswerte alte Hammerschmiede, eine ehemalige, heute liebevoll restaurierte Schleifmühle aus dem 19. Jahrhundert. Ein 1085 gegründetes Benediktinerkloster liegt ebenfalls in unmittelbarer Nähe; im Zuge der Reformation ging es an die Herzöge von Württemberg und beherbergt heute ein Gymnasium. Um die geheimnisvolle Quelle ranken sich mehrere Sagen und Legenden. Im Volksglauben hielt man sie für bodenlos, und bei jedem Versuch, mit einem Lot die Tiefe zu messen, hätte eine Nixe das Gewicht gestohlen. Außerdem sei die schöne Lau, so berichtet Eduard Mörike in einer Erzählung, in den Blautopf verbannt worden, weil sie nicht lachen konnte und ihrem Mann nur tote Kinder gebar.

The largest and deepest spring in Germany can be found in Blaubeuren at the foot of the Swabian Alb. It is known as the Blautopf ("Bowl of the Blau"); it is 21 meters (69 feet) deep and feeds the Blau, a river which flows into the Danube some 15 kilometers (9 miles) further on, in the built-up area of Ulm. Geologically speaking this is a karst spring, in other words a spring fed by water which has seeped into the ground elsewhere. The blue color is related to the water's high limestone content; the short-wave blue components of the light are scattered more strongly than the other colors. Near the Blautopf stands the ancient Hammerschmiede, a former grinding mill which has been lovingly restored and is worth a visit. The former Benedictine monastery founded in 1085 also lies in the vicinity; during the Reformation it was passed to the dukes of Württemberg and today houses a grammar school. In 1985, divers exploring the Blautopf discovered a vast network of caves with stalactites. The mysterious spring is the source of numerous myths and legends. Popular belief claimed that the spring was bottomless, and that at every attempt to measure its depth using a plumb line, a water sprite stole the weight. Writer-poet Eduard Mörike related in a short story how the beautiful water sprite Lau was banished to the Blautopf because she was incapable of laughing and only bore her husband stillborn children.

Die Quelle der Blau, der Blautopf in Blaubeuren, mit der alten Hammerschmiede.

The source of the Blau, the Blautopf in Blaubeuren, with the old Hammerschmiede grinding mill.

Aalen, Schwäbisch Gmünd, Göppingen

Aalen, Schwäbisch Gmünd, Göppingen

Links: Göppingen mit Hohenstaufen (684 m). Orgel im Heilig-Kreuz-Münster und Marienbrunnen, Schwäbisch Gmünd. Rechts unten: Marktplatz in Aalen.
Left: Göppingen with Hohenstaufen (684 m/ 2244 ft). The organ in the Cathedral of the Holy Cross and the Fountain of the Virgin Mary in Schwäbisch Gmünd. Bottom right: The market place in Aalen.

Die Römer bauten an der Stelle des heutigen Aalen 164 n. Chr. ein Kastell am Obergermanisch-Rätischen Limes, seit 2005 UNESCO-Welterbe. Das Limesmuseum Aalen befindet sich an einem Abschnitt dieser Grenzanlage. Das Wahrzeichen Schwäbisch Gmünds, das gotische Heilig-Kreuz-Münster, ist eine große Hallenkirche mit mächtigen Rundsäulen und einem sehr schönen Netzgewölbe. Die Kreisstadt Göppingen am Fuß der Schwäbischen Alb ist Liebhabern und Sammlern von Modelleisenbahnen bekannt als Sitz der Gebr. Märklin & Cie. GmbH. Oberhalb von Hohenstaufen, einem Stadtteil Göppingens, befindet sich die Burgruine Hohenstaufen, ein beliebtes Ausflugsziel.

In 164 A.D. the Romans built a fort on the Upper German-Raetian Limes on the site of present-day Aalen. It has been a UNESCO World Heritage site since 2005. The Limes Museum at Aalen lies along a section of the border fortifications. The main landmark of Schwäbisch Gmünd, the Gothic Cathedral of the Holy Cross, is a large hall church with massive round columns and very fine reticulated vaulting. The district town of Göppingen at the foot of the Swabian Alb is well-known to aficionados and collectors as the headquarters of Gebr. Märklin & Cie. GmbH. Above Hohenstaufen, a district of Göppingen, stands ruined Hohenstaufen castle.

SPECIAL | Land der Dichter und Denker

Land of poets and philosophers

Wiege des deutschen Idealismus …

Auf den Kunsthistoriker Eduard Paulus (1837–1907) geht der Spruch zurück: „Der Schiller und der Hegel,/ Der Schelling und der Hauff,/ Das ist bei uns die Regel,/ Das fällt hier gar nicht auf!" Für manche Ohren mag das arrogant klingen, zumal den meisten Schwaben das Sparbuch sicher mehr am Herzen liegt, als Hegels *Phänomenologie des Geistes*. Der Vierzeiler mag ironisch gemeint sein, ein bisschen Stolz schwingt schon mit. Immerhin: Der in Stuttgart geborene Georg Wilhelm Friedrich Hegel (1770–1831) gehört zusammen mit Friedrich Schelling (1775–1854), der in Leonberg zur Welt kam, zu den einflussreichsten Philosophen des Deutschen Idealismus. Beide haben in Tübingen Theologie studiert und waren zeitweise sogar Zimmergenossen im Tübinger Stift. Im 20. Jahrhundert war der im kleinen Schwarzwaldort Meßkirch geborene Martin Heidegger (1889–1976) einer der wichtigsten Denker, auch wenn seine Rolle im Nationalsozialismus noch immer kontrovers diskutiert wird. Universitätshochburgen sind bis heute Heidelberg, Tübingen und Freiburg.

The cradle of German Idealism …

The art historian Eduard Paulus (1837-1907) is credited with the saying: "Schiller and Hegel,/ Schelling and Hauff,/ Are two a penny here,/ So we hardly notice them!" Some people may think that sounds arrogant, given that most Swabians are more concerned about their savings account than Hegel's Phenomenology of Mind. But even if the little ditty was meant ironically, it still contains an element of pride. After all: Georg Wilhelm Friedrich Hegel (1770-1831), born in Stuttgart, belongs among the most influential philosophers of German Idealism, alongside Friedrich Schelling (1775-1854), who was born in Leonberg. They both studied theology in Tübingen and at one stage were even room-mates at the seminary there. During the twentieth century, Martin Heidegger (1889-1976), born in the little village of Messkirch in the Black Forest, was one of the country's leading philiosophers, even though his role in the National Socialist movement is still the subject of controversy. The universities of Heidelberg, Tübingen and Freiburg are bastions of learning to this day.

… und Heimat der Dichter

Auch die Liste der bedeutenden Dichter kann sich sehen lassen. Mit Friedrich Schiller (1759–1805) ist einer der beiden Klassiker der Deutschen Literatur ein Kind Württembergs. Er kam in Marbach am Neckar zur Welt, wo man 2009 auch seinen 250. Geburtstag feiert. Auf der Schillerhöhe über der Stadt, einem Park mit einem schönen Ausblick übers Neckartal, wurde bereits zu seinem 100. Geburtstag 1859 das Schillerdenkmal enthüllt. Heute befindet sich dort das Schiller-Nationalmuseum und das Literaturmuseum der Moderne. Der in Lauffen am Neckar geborene Friedrich Hölderlin (1770–1843) hat wohl einige der großartigsten Versdichtungen deutscher Sprache geschrieben; seine letzten Jahre verbrachte er in geistiger Umnachtung in Tübingen. In Stuttgart geboren ist Wilhelm Hauff (1802–1827), der ein beachtliches Werk hinterließ, obwohl er so jung – vermutlich an Typhus – starb. Unsterblich sind seine Märchenerzählungen, darunter „Kalif Storch", „Zwerg Nase", aber auch kritische Stoffe wie die Erzählung „Der Affe als Mensch" („Der junge Engländer").

… and home of poets

There is no shortage of poets here either. Friedrich Schiller (1759-1805), one of the two classical giants of German literature, was a native son of Württemberg. He was born in Marbach on the Neckar; the town will be celebrating his 250th birthday in 2009. The Schiller Monument was unveiled to mark his 100th birthday in 1859 on the Schillerhöhe above the town, a park with a lovely view across the Neckar valley. Today the town also boasts the Schiller National Museum and the Modern Literature Museum. Friedrich Hölderlin (1770-1843), born in Lauffen on the Neckar, wrote some of the most memorable poems in the German language; he spent his final years in a state of mental derangement in Tübingen. Wilhelm Hauff (1802-1827) was born in Stuttgart; he left an impressive oeuvre although he died very young, probably of typhoid. His fairy tales including Kalif Storch (Caliph Stork) and Zwerg Nase (Dwarf Long-Nose) are immortal, as are his critical works such as "Der Affe als Mensch" ("The Ape as Man"). The list of important poets is certainly an impressive one.

Links: Das anlässlich seines 100. Geburtstags errichtete Schillerdenkmal von 1859. Das Schiller-Nationalmuseum, Marbach am Neckar. Rechts: Schillers Geburtshaus (Mitte) in Marbach ist heute ein Museum.

Left: The statue of Schiller was erected to mark his 100th birthday in 1859. The Schiller National Museum in Marbach am Neckar. Right: Schiller's birthplace (center) in Marbach is now a museum.

Tübingen, Rottenburg und Reutlingen

Tübingen, Rottenburg and Reutlingen

Als „Tor zur Schwäbischen Alb" bezeichnet sich die Kreisstadt Reutlingen, etwa 20 Kilometer östlich von Tübingen. Bis 1802 war der Ort „Freie Reichsstadt", ein Status, der unter Kaiser Maximilian II., dessen Statue den um 1570 errichteten Marktbrunnen ziert, bestätigt wurde. Wer sich über die Entstehung der Schwäbischen Alb informieren möchte, dem ist ein Besuch im örtlichen Naturkundemuseum zu empfehlen. Wahrzeichen der Stadt ist die ab 1247 erbaute gotische Marienkirche mit ihrem 71 Meter hohen Turm, die seit der Reformation von der evangelischen Gemeinde genutzt wird. Westlich vor Tübingen lohnt ein Abstecher nach Rottenburg am Neckar, die Altstadt mit ihren engen Gassen ist besonders sehenswert. Die schwäbisch-alemannische Fasnet hat hier eine lange Tradition. In Tübingen ist das Leben geprägt von den Studenten, die ein Viertel der Einwohnerschaft stellen. Die Universitätsstadt am Neckar ist stolz auf die Dichter und Geistesgrößen, die hier gelebt haben, darunter Hölderlin, Schelling und Hegel. Eines der bekanntesten Bauwerke ist der am Neckarufer gelegene Hölderlinturm, in dem der psychisch kranke Dichter bis zu seinem Tod 1843 wohnte. Auf dem Neckar vor der Kulisse dieses Turms sind regelmäßig Stocherkähne unterwegs – die Art der Fortbewegung erinnert ein wenig an die Gondeln in Venedig. Unter Studenten beliebt sind Wettfahrten mit diesen Booten.

The large district town of Reutlingen calls itself the "Gateway to the Swabian Alb"; it lies some 20 kilometers (13 miles) east of Tübingen. Until 1802 it was a "Free Imperial city", a status which was confirmed under Emperor Maximilian II, whose statue adorns the market fountain erected in 1570. If you are interested in the formation of the Swabian Alb, you should plan a visit to the local Museum of Natural History. The town's landmark is the Gothic Church of the Virgin Mary. Construction began in 1247; the spire soars to a height of 71 meters (233 feet). Since the Reformation it has been used by the Protestant community. Before reaching Tübingen it is worth making a detour to the west to Rottenburg am Neckar, where the historic town center with its narrow alleys is particularly worth seeing. The Swabian-Alemannic Fasnet carnival has a long tradition here. Life in Tübingen is largely determined by the students, who make up a quarter of the town's inhabitants. The university town on the Neckar is proud of the poets and scholars who studied here, including Hölderlin, Schelling and Hegel. One of the most famous buildings is the Hölderlinturm on the banks of the Neckar, the tower in which the mentally ill poet lived until his death in 1843. Punts can still regularly be seen on the river in front of the tower. Students like to stage races in the shallow boats which bear a resemblance to the gondolas of Venice.

In diesem gelben Turm verbrachte der psychisch kranke Dichter Friedrich Hölderlin seine letzten Lebensjahre. Auf dem Neckar sind Stocherkähne zu sehen.

Mentally ill, the poet Friedrich Hölderlin spent his last years in this yellow tower. Punts can be seen on the Neckar.

Der Bodensee, das Allgäu und Oberschwaben

Lake Constance, Allgäu and Upper Swabia

Der größte Teil des deutschen Bodenseeufers liegt in Baden-Württemberg – ein kleiner Teil mit Lindau als Zentrum in Bayern. Das „Schwäbische Meer" ist umsäumt von historisch bedeutenden Städten: In Friedrichshafen steht die Wiege der Zeppeline, in Meersburg lebte und starb die Dichterin Annette von Droste-Hülshoff, Konstanz schrieb im 15. Jahrhundert europäische Geschichte mit seinem Konzil und im Pfahlbaumuseum in Unteruhldingen wird die Stein- und Bronzezeit lebendig.

Most of the German section of the shoreline of Lake Constance lies in Baden-Württemberg; a shorter section, lies in Bavaria. The lake is bordered by historically important towns: Friedrichshafen is the birthplace of the zeppelin; Meersburg was the town were the poetess Annette von Droste-Hülshoff lived and died; and in the 15th century Konstanz earned a place in the history of Europe with the Council of Constance.

Ravensburg, Wangen und Biberach

Ravensburg, Wangen and Biberach

Die hügelige Landschaft zwischen Schwäbischer Alb, Donau und Bodensee wird als Oberschwaben bezeichnet. Wichtige Städte sind hier Biberach an der Riß, Ravensburg und Wangen im Allgäu. Biberach ist bekannt als eine der Stationen der im Volkslied verewigten „Schwäbischen Eisenbahn", die tatsächlich Mitte des 19. Jahrhunderts als erste durchgehende Strecke Stuttgart und Friedrichshafen verbunden hat. Die Riß ist ein Nebenfluss der Donau, nach ihr wurde die vorletzte Eiszeit vor 230 000 bis 130 000 Jahren benannt. Neben zahlreichen schönen Fachwerkbauten ist das Ulmer Tor, das letzte erhaltene Tor der mittelalterlichen Stadtbefestigung, ein beliebtes Fotomotiv. Wangen im Allgäu gilt als Stadt der Brunnen, von denen der hübsche Ort 25 aufweisen kann. Ein besonders originelles Exemplar ist der Amtsschimmelbrunnen (1984) auf dem Platz vor dem Landratsamt. Wahrzeichen der Stadt ist das reich bemalte spätgotische Ravensburger Tor. Ravensburg selbst, etwa 25 Kilometer nordwestlich von Wangen gelegen, zeichnet sich durch seine vielen Türme aus, deren bekanntester der 51 Meter hohe Mehlsack ist, das Wahrzeichen der Stadt. Die Altstadt, da im Zweiten Weltkrieg weitgehend verschont, ist fast vollständig erhalten, besonders auffallend ist das Rathaus und das ehemalige Münz- und Eichamt, das sogenannte Waaghaus. Ravensburg gehört zu den Hochburgen der schwäbisch-alemannischen Fasnet.

The hilly region between the Swabian Alb, the Danube, and Lake Constance is known as Upper Swabia. The important towns here are Biberach an der Riss, Ravensburg and Wangen im Allgäu. Biberach is famous as one of the stations on the "Swabian Railway", immortalized in a folk song. In the mid-nineteenth century it was indeed the first continuous stretch, linking Stuttgart and Friedrichshafen. The Riss is a tributary of the Danube and gave its name to the penultimate Ice Age which occurred some 230,000 to 130,000 years ago. The numerous attractive timbered buildings are popular subjects for photographs, as is also the Ulmer Tor, the last remaining gateway of the medieval town fortifications. Pretty Wangen im Allgäu is known as the "Town of Fountains"; it boasts 25 of them – particularly original is the "Amtsschimmel"-fountain (Red-Tape-fountain). The town's landmark is the elaborately painted late Gothic Ravensburger Tor, another historic gateway. Ravensburg itself lies some 25 kilometers (16 miles) northwest of Wangen. Its distinguishing feature is its numerous towers; the most famous is the Mehlsack, 51 meters (167 feet) tall and the town's landmark. The historic town center has survived World War II almost undamaged. Of particular note are the Town Hall and the former Mint and Weights and Measures Office, the so-called Waaghaus. Ravensburg is also one of the main centers of Fasnet.

Seite 40, 41: Wasserburg am Bodensee. Schloss Mainau. Pirmin-Statue, Insel Reichenau. Abendstimmung mit Rheintorturm und Münster, Konstanz. Bodensee, Rhein bei Konstanz, Luftbild.

Page 40, 41: Wasserburg on Lake Constance. Mainau Castle. Statue of monk-bishop Pirmin on the island of Reichenau. Evening mood with the Rheintor tower and the cathedral in Konstanz. Lake Constance, the Rhine near Konstanz, seen from the air.

Von links oben im Uhrzeigersinn: Altstadt mit Lederhaus und Stadt-
übersicht, Ravensburg. Herrenstraße in Wangen im Allgäu. Marktplatz in Biberach mit Kirche St. Martin.

*From left, clockwise: The historic town center in Ravensburg with
the Lederhaus and a town plan. Herrenstrasse in Wangen im Allgäu.
The market place in Biberach with St. Martin's Church.*

Zeppelinstadt
Friedrichshafen

Zeppelin town Friedrichshafen

Mit der Bodenseestadt Friedrichshafen ist die Entwicklung der Luftschiffe, die nach ihrem Erfinder Ferdinand Graf von Zeppelin auch „Zeppeline" genannt werden, eng verbunden. Am 2. Juli 1900 hob dort das erste lenkbare mit Gas gefüllte Starrluftschiff vom Boden ab. Zu Beginn waren die Luftschiffe den ersten Flugzeugen technisch überlegen: Sie waren fast genauso schnell, hatten eine wesentlich größere Reichweite und konnten höhere Nutzlasten befördern. In ihrer Ausstattung glichen sie fliegenden Hotels. Nach dem Ersten Weltkrieg wurden sie im Transatlantikflugverkehr eingesetzt. Einen vorläufigen Schlussstrich unter diese Technologie zog jedoch die Katastrophe von Lakehurst am 6. Mai 1937, bei der die mit 200 000 Kubikmetern Wasserstoff gefüllte LZ 129 Hindenburg innerhalb weniger Sekunden in Flammen aufging. Erst in jüngster Zeit werden wieder Luftschiffe gebaut, allerdings eher für Werbezwecke oder den Tourismus. Das Zeppelinmuseum am Hafen dokumentiert die Geschichte der „fliegenden Zigarren". Von Friedrichshafen aus sind mit den Schiffen der „Weißen Flotte" die meisten anderen Bodenseestädte erreichbar.

The development of the airships which were named "Zeppelins" after their inventor Count Ferdinand von Zeppelin, is closely linked to Friedrichshafen, a town on Lake Constance. The first dirigible gas-filled rigid airship took to the air here on July 2, 1900. Initially, airships were technically superior to the first aircraft: they were almost as fast, had a considerably greater range and could carry heavier loads. They were fitted out like flying hotels, and after World War I they were used for transatlantic flights. The technology was temporarily abandoned, however, following the Lakehurst catastrophe of May 6, 1937, during which LZ 129 Hindenburg containing 200,000 cubic meters of hydrogen was engulfed in a matter of seconds in a huge ball of flame. Only in recent years has the construction of airships been resumed, albeit nowadays mostly for advertising purposes or for tourist use. The Zeppelin Museum beside the port presents an impressive history of the "flying cigars." From Friedrichshafen you can also take the steamers of the "White Fleet" to most other towns on Lake Constance.

Namensgeber der Stadt am Nordufer des Bodensees war König Friedrich I. von Württemberg, der 1811 die ehemalige Reichsstadt Buchhorn mit dem Dorf und dem Kloster Hofen zusammenlegte. Wirtschaftlich profitierte die Stadt von diesem Zusammenschluss. Friedrichshafen wurde ein bedeutender Freihafen und Warenumschlagplatz im Handel mit der Schweiz. Mit dem König siedelten sich auch bald hohe Beamte und Minister an, die der Stadt

Wohlstand brachten. Die von dem Barockbaumeister Michael Beer zwischen 1654 und 1661 erbaute, ab 1697 durch Christian Thumb erweiterte Klosteranlage wurde Anfang des 19. Jahrhunderts zu einem Schloss umgebaut und diente den württembergischen Königen als Sommerresidenz. Heute wird es von der württembergischen Herzogsfamilie bewohnt. Weithin sichtbar sind die beiden 55 Meter hohen Türme der barocken Schlosskirche mit ihren Zwiebeldächern. Die Prioriatskirche St. Andreas des ehemaligen Benediktinerklosters Hofen ist neben dem Zeppelin Wahrzeichen der Bodenseestadt. Sie wurde von Christian Thumb zwischen 1695 und 1702 an der Stelle einer älteren Klosterkirche errichtet.

The town of Friedrichshafen on the north shore of Lake Constance was named for King Friedrich I of Württemberg, who amalgamated the former Imperial City of Buchhorn with the village and monastery of Hofen in 1811. It profited economically from the amalgamation. Friedrichshafen became an important free port and trading center with Switzerland. Senior officials and ministers followed the king and settled in the town, bringing prosperity. The monastery complex, built by Baroque master architect Michael Beer between 1654 and 1661 and extended by Christian Thumb in 1697, was converted into a palace at the beginning of the nineteenth century, serving the kings of Württemberg as a summer residence. Today it is the home of the Dukes of Württemberg. The towers of the Baroque palace church with their onion towers are 55 meters (180 feet) high and can be seen from a distance. The former monastery church of Hofen Monastery is used by the Protestant community and is the town's second landmark, beside the zeppelin. It was built by Christian Thumb between 1695 and 1702 on the site of an older monastery church.

Der im September 2000 eingeweihte Aussichtsturm in Friedrichshafen ist über 22 Meter hoch und frei zugänglich.

Inaugurated in September 2000, the observation tower in Friedrichshafen is over 22 meters (72 feet) tall and open to the public.

Konstanz, das Tor zur Schweiz

Konstanz, the Gateway to Switzerland

Die neun Meter hohe Imperia von Peter Lenk in der Hafeneinfahrt von Konstanz weist ironisch auf ein geschichtliches Großereignis, das bis heute mit dem Namen der Stadt verbunden ist: das Konstanzer Konzil von 1414 bis 1418. Das Konzilsgebäude, in dem das Konklave zur Papstwahl stattfand, befindet sich noch heute am Bodenseeufer. Die katholische Kirche war damals in einem beklagenswerten Zustand: Die Spaltung drohte, zwei Päpste stritten um die Macht. Nach zähem Ringen einigte man sich auf einen dritten, Martin V. Das Großereignis führte viele weltliche und geistliche Würdenträger mitsamt ihrem Gefolge in die Stadt – darunter auch zahlreiche Prostituierte. Darauf spielt die 1993 errichtete Statue an, eine leicht geschürzte Kurtisane, zwei nackte, kleine Gauklerfiguren mit den Insignien von Kaiser und Papst in ihren Händen. Doch man findet auch traditionellere Darstellungen des Ereignisses, so zum Beispiel die Bilderfolge an der Fassade am Haus zum Hohen Hafen. Bei einem Rundgang durch die schmucke Innenstadt fällt – neben vielen anderen historischen Gebäuden – das neue Rathaus mit seinem im Renaissancestil umgebauten Innenhof ins Auge. Das romanische Münster Unserer Lieben Frau diente während des Konzils als Sitzungssaal. Über die Jahre ist Konstanz mit der Schweizer Nachbarstadt Kreuzlingen zusammengewachsen – die Grenze verläuft heute mitten durch die Stadt.

Peter Lenk's statue Imperia, nine meters (30 feet) high, stands in the harbor entrance of Konstanz and refers ironically to a major historical event which is still linked to this day with the name of the town: the Council of Constance (1414-1418). The Council building, in which the conclave to elect the Pope was held, still stands on the shores of the lake. The Catholic Church was in a pitiful state at that time. It was on the verge of splitting into two factions, and two Popes were both struggling to gain power. After a hard-fought contest the decision was taken in favor of a third, Martin V. The Council brought numerous secular and ecclesiastical dignitaries with their entourages to town – including a large number of prostitutes. The statue, erected in 1993, refers to this fact, showing as it does the scantily-clad courtesans and two small, naked traveling entertainers bearing the insignia of the Emperor and the Pope. But Konstanz also offers more traditional representations of the world-famous event, including the series of pictures on the façade of the Haus zum Hohen Hafen. During a tour of the pretty city center you are certain to notice – among the many other historic buildings – the new Town Hall with its Renaissance-style inner courtyard. Incidentally the Romanesque Cathedral of the Virgin Mary was used as a conference room during the Council. Konstanz has grown together with its Swiss neighbor, Kreuzlingen.

Von links oben im Uhrzeigersinn: Die mächtige Imperia-Statue in der Hafeneinfahrt erinnert an das Konstanzer Konzil; Rathaus, Innenhof. Altstadthaus. Rheintorturm.

Clockwise from top left: The mighty statue of Imperia in the entrance to the harbor recalls the Council of Constance; Town Hall, the inner courtyard. A house in the historic town center. The Rheintor tower.

SPECIAL | Oberschwäbisches Barock

Upper Swabian Baroque

Pracht und Prunk der Gegenreformation

Nach dem Dreißigjährigen Krieg, als Städte und Dörfer, aber auch die Sakralbauten verwüstet wurden, kam es zu einer besonders regen Bautätigkeit. Der Zeitgeschmack forderte Prunk, für die absolutistischen Fürsten war es Demonstration ihrer Macht, für die katholische Gegenreformation der Versuch, die Gläubigen zu halten oder zurückzugewinnen. Im Süden betraf die sinnlich mitreißende Prunkentfaltung hauptsächlich Klöster und Kirchen. Viele Äbte ließen derart verschwenderische Bauwerke errichten, dass sich die Kosten überschlugen, einige der Kirchenmänner sogar zum Abdanken zwang. Der barocke Stil kam aus Italien zu uns – für Bildhauer und Architekten war deshalb der anregende Aufenthalt bei dem südlichen Nachbarn wesentlicher Teil der Lehrzeit. Die neue Bauart löste die strengere Formensprache der Renaissance ab und führte runde, konkave und konvexe, schwingende Gestaltungselemente ein. Ornamentale Strukturen wurden häufig eingesetzt und dienten der Steigerung der Wirkung. Im Barock entwickelte sich das Gebäude zu einem Gesamtkunstwerk – Architekten, Stuckatoren, Bildhauer und Maler schufen ein Ensemble, in dem Malerei und Skulptur, Lichteffekte, edle Materialien – vor allem Gold und Marmor – eine wichtige Rolle spielten. In Oberschwaben kam dieser Stil erst Ende des 17. Jahrhunderts an. Eines der schönsten Beispiele ist hier die dem Spätbarock zugeordnete Kloster- und Wallfahrtskirche Birnau am Bodensee (1750), das Hauptwerk des Vorarlberger Barockbaumeisters Peter Thumb. Die Klosterkirche der ehemaligen Abtei Salem, ein reichsunmittelbares Zisterzienserkloster, zählt zu den Hauptsehenswürdigkeiten der Oberschwäbischen Barockstraße. Der üppig gestaltete Innenraum präsentiert sich wie ein Festsaal. Hochaltar und viele der Skulpturen sind das Werk Joseph Anton Feuchtmayers (1692–1770), darunter der berühmte „Honigschlecker", ein Honig naschender Engel, der für Lebenslust steht und als Schutzengel der Liebenden gilt. Die ehemalige Reichsabtei Ochsenhausen wurde damals ebenfalls im barocken Stil umgebaut (1725–1732). Die nach Entwürfen von Franz Beer erbaute Basilika St. Martin von Weingarten bei Ravensburg (1715–1724) gilt als die größte Barockkirche nördlich der Alpen.

Die Wallfahrtskirche Birnau (1750) am Bodensee zählt zu den schönsten Bauwerken des oberschwäbischen Barock.

The pilgrimage church of Birnau (1750) on Lake Constance is one of the finest examples of the Upper Swabian Baroque style.

The splendor of the Counter-Reformation

The Thirty Years' War, which devastated towns, villages and monasteries, was followed by a period of lively building activity. Contemporary taste demanded splendor; for the absolute rulers it was a demonstration of their might, and for the Catholic Counter-Reformation it represented an attempt to keep the faithful or to win them back. In the south the sensuous blossoming of pomp and circumstance mostly affected the monasteries and churches. Many abbots had such extravagant buildings erected that the costs got out of control and some of them even had to resign because of it. The Baroque style reached Germany from Italy, and for sculptors and architects an inspiring stay south of the Alps became an important part of their apprenticeship. The new style replaced the stricter language of form of the Renaissance, introducing round, concave and convex arching design elements. The ornamentation became important and served to increase the effect. The Baroque building became a complete work of art as architects, stucco experts, sculptors and painters created an ensemble in which painting and sculpture, light effects and noble materials – especially gold and marble – played an important part. This fashion did not arrive in Upper Swabia until the end of the seventeenth century. One of the loveliest examples is the late Baroque monastery and pilgrimage church of Birnau on Lake Constance (1750), the principal work of the Baroque master builder Peter Thumb (1681-1766). The monastery church of the former Imperial abbey of Salem, a Cistercian abbey which enjoyed the privilege of Imperial immediacy, is one of the principal sights on the Upper Swabian Baroque Road. The magnificent interior looks like a banqueting hall. The high altar and many of the sculptures are the work of Joseph Anton Feuchtmayer (1692-1770), including the famous "Honigschlecker", an angel eating honey which represents joie-de-vivre and is regarded as the guardian angel of lovers. The former Imperial abbey of Ochsenhausen was also rebuilt in the Baroque style at the time (1725-1732). The Baroque Basilica of St. Martin in Weingarten near Ravensburg (1715-1724) was built according to the design of Franz Beer and is the largest Baroque church north of the Alps.

Das mächtige Barockkloster in Ochsenhausen war ursprünglich eine Benediktinerabtei. Heute beherbergt es neben einem Museum eine Musikakademie.

The massive Baroque monastery in Ochsenhausen was originally a Benedictine abbey. Today it houses a museum and a music academy.

Meersburg, Überlingen, Mainau und Reichenau

Meersburg, Überlingen, Mainau and Reichenau

Das spätgotische Alte Schloss, die Meersburg mit dem Dagobertsturm, erkennbar an seinem Staffelgiebel, bildet das Zentrum der Stadt am Nordufer des Bodensees. Meersburg war die Wahlheimat der Dichterin Annette von Droste-Hülshoff (1797–1848), ihr Sterbezimmer befindet sich im Alten Schloss und kann im Rahmen eines Rundgangs besichtigt werden. Da der alte Bau den Repräsentationsvorstellungen späterer Fürsten nicht mehr genügte, wurde Anfang des 18. Jahrhunderts das Neue Schloss errichtet, an dem der bedeutende Barockbaumeister Balthasar Neumann maßgeblich mitwirkte. Überlingen am nordwestlichen Zweigbecken des Sees ist die Wahlheimat des in Wasserburg geborenen Schriftstellers Martin Walser. Unbedingt sehenswert sind die schöne Altstadt und das spätgotische Münster St. Nikolas mit seinem imposanten Altar. Nur etwa 45 Hektar umfasst die Insel Mainau im Überlinger See, die der aus Schweden stammende Graf Bernadotte (1909–2004) in ein Blumenparadies verwandelt hat. Mit seiner Grünen Charta von 1961 legte er das erste Umweltschutzprogramm in der Geschichte der Bundesrepublik vor. Fast zwei Millionen Besucher lassen sich Jahr für Jahr von dieser Pracht bezaubern. Die Insel Reichenau im Untersee ist die größte Bodenseeinsel; seit 2000 steht sie auf der UNESCO-Liste des Weltkulturerbes. Das Kloster wurde 724 von dem Mönchsbischof Pirmin gegründet.

The late Gothic Old Castle forms the center of the town on the northern shore of Lake Constance. It overlooks Meersburg with its Dagobert Tower and is recognizable for its stepped gable. Meersburg as the elective home of the poetess Annette von Droste-Hülshoff (1797-1848); the room in which she died is in the Old Castle and can be visited during a guided tour. Since the old building no longer met the representative requirements of later princes, the New Castle was built in the early eighteenth century. Baroque master builder Balthasar Neumann played an important part in its design. Überlingen, on the northwest branch of the lake, is famous as the elective home of writer Martin Walser, who was born in Wasserburg. The lovely old town and the late-Gothic St. Nicholas' Cathedral with its imposing altar are definitely worth seeing. Lying in the Überlinger See, the island of Mainau only covers an area of approximately 45 hectares (111 acres). Count Bernadotte (1909-2004) from Sweden transformed it into a floral paradise. His Green Charter of 1961 was the first environmental protection program in the history of the Federal Republic. Almost two million visitors every year are enchanted by the floral magnificence. Reichenau in the Untersee is the largest of the islands in Lake Constance; since 2000 it has been on the UNESCO World Heritage List. The monastery was founded in 724 by the monk-bishop Pirmin.

Von links oben im Uhrzeigersinn: Luftbild der Insel Mainau. Die alte Meersburg mit dem Dagobertsturm, Meersburg. Blühende Wiese auf der Insel Mainau. Stiftskirche St. Georg, Insel Reichenau.

Clockwise from top left: An aerial view of the island of Mainau. The Old Castle with the Dagobert Tower in Meersburg. A meadow in full bloom on the island of Mainau. The Collegiate Church of St. George on the island of Reichenau.

Pfahlbausiedlung
Unteruhldingen
Stilted settlement Unteruhldingen

Das ganzjährig geöffnete archäologische Freilichtmuseum Unteruhlding liegt am Nordufer des Überlinger Sees gegenüber der Insel Mainau. Im Museum erfährt man anschaulich, wie die Menschen in der Stein- und Bronzezeit (zwischen 4000 und 850 v. Chr.) gelebt haben. An manchen Wochenenden schlüpft einer der Museumsmitarbeiter in die Rolle eines Steinzeitmenschen und demonstriert, wie mühevoll es damals war, Werkzeuge herzustellen oder Feuer zu machen. Auch die Ergebnisse eines Filmprojekts des SWR 2007, bei dem 13 Personen für acht Wochen unter steinzeitlichen Bedingungen lebten, werden im Museum dokumentiert.

The open-air archeological museum of Unteruhlding is open all the year round. It lies on the north shore of the Überlinger See opposite the island of Mainau. The museum provides an interesting account of how people lived during the Stone and Bronze Ages (between 4000 and 850 B.C.). Some weekends one of the museum staff takes on the role of a Stone Age man and demonstrates how arduous it was then to make tools or light a fire – an experience not only for children. In 2007, as part of a film project produced by SWR, thirteen people lived under Stone Age conditions for eight weeks in very cramped quarters – an experiment whose results have been documented in the museum.

Pfahlbauten im Freilicht-museum in Unteruhldingen am Bodensee.

Stilted buildings in the open-air museum in Unteruhldingen on Lake Constance.

Schwarzwald und die Oberrheinische Tiefebene

The Black Forest and the Plain of the Upper Rhine

Als „typisch deutsch" gilt im Ausland oft auch das Schwarzwaldmädel mit dem Bollenhut, der aber so eigentlich nur in drei Dörfern gebräuchlich ist. Die dicht bewaldete Mittelgebirgslandschaft zwischen Karlsruhe und Lörrach bietet jedoch wesentlich mehr: Sie ist ideal für Wanderungen, im Winter fürs Skifahren, ein Dorado für Genießer. Immerhin befinden sich hier zwei der neun deutschen Dreisternelokale – beide in der Schwarzwaldgemeinde Baiersbronn.

Among the popular cliché images of Germany abroad is the Black Forest girl with the straw hat decorated with bobbles, which is actually only worn in three Black Forest villages. The densely forested range of medium-altitude mountains between Karlsruhe and Lörrach can offer more than this, however. It is an ideal countryside for hiking or for skiing in winter, and is a gourmet's paradise: after all, two of Germany's nine three-star restaurants are here, in Baiersbronn.

Karlsruhe und der Nordschwarzwald

Karlsruhe and the Northern Black Forest

Ein Traum des Markgrafen Karl-Wilhelm von Baden-Durlach soll der Legende nach zur Gründung von Karlsruhe geführt haben. Er sah ein prachtvolles Schloss und eine Stadt, deren Straßen wie ein Fächer um das Schloss angeordnet waren – 1715 beschloss er, diese Anlage zu bauen. Karlsruhe avancierte bald zur Haupt- und Residenzstadt Badens. In den Medien steht Karlsruhe meist für das Bundesverfassungsgericht, das dort seinen Sitz hat. Stolz ist die Stadt auch auf ihre Technische Universität – 1825 gegründet und damit die älteste ihrer Art in Deutschland. Nicht versäumen sollte man einen Besuch im Zentrum für Kunst und Medientechnologie (ZKM), weltweit die größte Einrichtung für Medienkunst. Südöstlich von Karlsruhe liegt die Goldstadt Pforzheim, bekannt durch ihre Schmuckindustrie. In Pforzheim wurde der Humanist Johannes Reuchlin (1455–1522) geboren, der eine Lateinschule gründete, zu dessen Schülern auch der im nahe gelegenen Bretten geborene Lutherfreund Philipp Melanchthon gehörte. Bretten selbst führt den Mops, das „Brettener Hundle", als Wahrzeichen. Der Sage nach schickte man 1504 während einer Belagerung einen gemästeten Mops vor die Stadt, der vortäuschen sollte, dass an Nahrung kein Mangel herrsche, eine Belagerung mit dem Ziel des Aushungerns also zwecklos wäre. Die List wirkte, die Belagerer schnitten dem fetten Hund den Schwanz ab und zogen von dannen.

According to legend, one of Margrave Karl-Wilhelm von Baden-Durlach's dreams resulted in the founding of Karlsruhe. He saw a magnificent castle and a town whose streets were arranged in a fan shape around the castle; and in 1715 he decided to build the settlement he had seen. Karlsruhe soon became the capital of Baden, and the seat of the ruling family. When Karlsruhe is mentioned in the media these days it is usually in connection with the Federal Constitutional Court, which has its headquarters here. The town is also proud of its renowned Technical University, founded in 1825 and thus the oldest of its kind in Germany. Visitors should not miss the centre of art and media (ZKM). The "Gold Town" of Pforzheim lies to the southeast of Karlsruhe; it is famous for the jewelry industry. The philosopher and humanist Johannes Reuchlin (1455-1522) was born there; he founded a grammar school whose pupils included Philipp Melanchthon, the friend of Luther, who was born in nearby Bretten. Bretten itself has as its heraldic dog the pug, also known as the "Brettener Hundle." According to legend a pug which had been deliberately fattened up was sent out in 1504 during a siege to try to deceive the enemy into thinking that there was no shortage of food in the town, and that a siege with the aim of starving the citizens was pointless. The trick worked; the besieging army cut off the dog's tail and moved on.

Seite 54, 55: Blick auf den Schluchsee bei St. Blasien, Schwarzwald. Schloss Gottesaue, Karlsruhe, heute Musikhochschule. Schwabentor in Freiburg i. Br. Winterstimmung in Königsfeld, Schwarzwald.

Page 54, 55: A view of Lake Schluchsee, near St. Blasien in the Black Forest. Gottesaue Castle in Karlsruhe, now a music school. The Schwabentor in Freiburg im Breisgau. Winter mood in Königsfeld in the Black Forest.

Blick vom Schlossturm auf den Schlossplatz in Karlsruhe.
Die Stadt wurde fächerförmig um das Schloss erbaut.

The view from the castle tower on Castle Square in Karlsruhe.
The town was laid out around the castle in the shape of a fan.

Baden-Baden, Rastatt und Offenburg

Baden-Baden, Rastatt and Offenburg

Zu den berühmtesten Gästen des Spielkasinos Baden-Baden gehörte zweifellos der russische Schriftsteller Dostojewski, der seine Spielsucht in seinem Roman „Der Spieler" thematisierte. Doch er war nicht der einzige Gast aus dem Zarenreich: Turgenew nimmt in seinem Roman „Rauch" (1867) das Leben der russischen Adeligen im vornehmen Baden-Baden aufs Korn. Traditionell trafen sich hier Boheme und Adel aus ganz Europa. Auch der französische Komponist Hector Berlioz war regelmäßiger Gast, mit seiner hier uraufgeführten Opéra comique „Béatrice et Bénédict" wurde 1862 das neu errichtete Theater eröffnet. Der Kurort steht inzwischen längst auch Normalsterblichen offen, und im Kasino kann man heute wie damals viel Geld gewinnen – oder verlieren. Eine Hauptattraktion ist die Staatliche Kunsthalle mit ihren mehrmals im Jahr wechselnden überregional bedeutsamen Ausstellungen, 2009 feiert sie ihr 100-jähriges Bestehen. Direkt verbunden mit der Kunsthalle ist das 2004 eröffnete Museum Frieder Burda mit moderner Kunst von Pablo Picasso bis Gerhard Richter.

One of the most illustrious visitors to the casino at Baden-Baden was without doubt the Russian writer Fyodor Dostoevsky, who described his addiction to gambling in his novel The Gambler. But he was not the only guest from the Tsarist Empire: in his novel Smoke (1867), Turgenev satirizes the life of Russian aristocracy in the otherwise oh-so-genteel Baden-Baden. According to tradition, artists and aristocracy from all over Europe met here. The French composer Hector Berlioz was a regular guest; the première of his opéra comique Béatrice et Bénédict was also the opening performance at the newly-built theatre in 1862. Nowadays the spa is also accessible to normal mortals; as in former times, you can still win large sums of money – or lose them – in the casino today. One of the main attractions is the Staatliche Kunsthalle, the state art gallery which presents several changing exhibitions of national importance each year; in 2009 it will also be celebrating its centenary. Directly linked to the Kunsthalle is the Museum Frieder Burda, opened in 2004 and displaying modern art from Pablo Picasso to Gerhard Richter.

Schöne Fachwerk-häuser in Offen-burg.

Fine timbered buildings in Offenburg.

Eine Jupiterfigur schleudert Blitze, und das nicht in Griechenland, sondern vom Dach des Residenzschlosses in Rastatt aus. Erbaut von Markgraf Ludwig Wilhelm von Baden (1655–1707), einem Spross der älteren markgräflichen Linie, die mit ihm ausstarb, war das Schloss von 1707 bis 1771 markgräfliche Residenz. Ludwig Wilhelm war zu Lebzeiten wegen seiner militärischen Erfolge in den Türkenkriegen, besonders bei der Befreiung Wiens (1683), als „Türkenlouis" bekannt. Seit 1693 musste er sich gegen die Franzosen wehren, die sich rechtsrheinisch ausgebreitet hatten – wahrscheinlich ist das der Grund, warum Jupiters Blitze gegen Straßburg gerichtet sind. Auch hier war er allerdings siegreich und konnte die verlorenen Gebiete 1697 wieder zurückerobern. Noch etwas weiter südlich gelangt man zur großen Kreisstadt Offenburg, die im Weinbaugebiet Baden liegt. Sehenswert ist hier besonders die Heilig-Kreuz-Kirche, die 1791 geweiht wurde und deren Innenraum fast vollständig ausgemalt ist. Etwa neun Kilometer südöstlich befinden wir uns in Gengenbach, einer Weinbaugemeinde, die für ihre zahlreichen Türme berühmt ist.

A statue of Jupiter casts its thunderbolt, not in Greece, but from the roof of the palace residence in Rastatt. Built by Margrave Ludwig Wilhelm von Baden (1655-1707) the palace served as aristocratic residence from 1707 until 1771, when this line of the family died out. During his lifetime Ludwig Wilhelm was known as "Türkenlouis" because of his military success during the wars against the Turks, especially the liberation of Vienna (1683). From 1693 he had to defend himself against the French, who had spread out along the right bank of the Rhine; that is probably the reason why Jupiter's thunderbolts seem to be aimed towards Strasbourg. Here, too, he was victorious and in 1697 succeeded in winning back the territory conquered by the French. A little further south you will arrive in Offenburg, which lies in Baden's wine-growing area. Particularly worth seeing here is the Church of the Holy Cross, consecrated in 1791 and boasting an interior which is almost completely covered with paintings. Some nine kilometers (6 miles) to the southeast we reach Gengenbach, a wine-growing community which is famous for its numerous towers.

SPECIAL | Weinregion Baden-Württemberg

The wineland of Baden-Württemberg

Den Hängen und Steillagen abgetrotzt

Württemberg ist traditionell ein Rotweingebiet. Die vorherrschende Traube ist der Trollinger, ein leichter, frischer Rotwein. Weitere wichtige Trauben sind der Schwarzriesling und der etwas anspruchsvollere Lemberger. Letzterer ergibt tanninreichere, dunklere Weine und wird gern im Faß ausgebaut. Ein guter Lemberger kann durchaus mit einem Burgunder mithalten. Gern werden Trollinger und Lemberger miteinander verschnitten, und wenn es geschickt gemacht wird, kommt so das Beste beider Geschmacksrichtungen zur Geltung. An Weißweinsorten gibt es hier in geringerem Maße: den Riesling, die deutsche Traube schlechthin, und den Kerner, eine Kreuzung von Riesling und Trollinger. Der meiste Wein wird im Land selbst getrunken, die besten Lagen sind nicht groß genug für den Export. Versuche einer breiteren Vermarktung in der Vergangenheit – das Motto lautet bis heute „Kenner trinken Württemberger" – haben eine Zeit lang zu einer Qualitätseinbuße geführt. Heute besinnt man sich wieder auf die kleineren, sorgfältig ausgebauten Lagen, und damit auf Qualität.

Won from the slopes and steep locations

Traditionally, Württemberg is a red-wine area. The most commonly grown grape is the Trollinger, which produces a light, fresh red wine. Other important grape varieties here are the Schwarzriesling and the somewhat more demanding Lemberger. The latter produces darker wines rich in tannin; they are often matured in barrels. A good Lemberger can compete with a Burgundy wine. The two red-wine varieties are often blended together; if it is skillfully done, the best characteristics of both are shown to good advantage. Other wine varieties here include, to a lesser extent, the Riesling, Germany's most typical grape variety, and the Kerner, a cross between Riesling and Trollinger. Most of the wine produced is drunk locally; the best locations are too small to export much. Past attempts at a broader marketing – the motto to this day remains "Connoisseurs drink Württemberg wines" – led for a while to a reduction in quality. Today more emphasis is placed once more on the smaller, more carefully cultivated locations, and thus on quality.

*Weinlese in Stuttgart Burk-
heim, Kaiserstuhl. Rechts:
Oberrotweil, Kaiserstuhl.
Vintage in Stuttgart. Wine
village Burkheim and Oberrotweil, Kaiserstuhl.*

Baden – von der Sonne verwöhnt

Der Weinbau im klimatisch wesentlich begüns-
tigteren Baden setzt andere Schwerpunkte. Die
Landschaft zwischen Karlsruhe, Baden-Baden bis
zum Kaiserstuhl zählt zu den wärmsten Regionen
Deutschlands. Hier gedeihen primär Weißwein-
reben, leichte, wie der Müller-Thurgau oder der
Silvaner, gehaltvollere wie der Ruländer. Auch der
Riesling wird hier angebaut. Beliebt sind darüber
hinaus die Weißherbste, leicht moussierende Rosé-
weine. Bei den Rotweinen sind es hauptsächlich
Spätburgunder und der Schwarzriesling. In Baden
steht die Wiege der deutschen Ökologiebewegung.
Entsprechend haben sich auch die Prinzipien eines
biologischen Anbaus auf breiter Ebene durchge-
setzt. Zum badischen Weinanbaugebiet zählt auch
die Insel Reichenau im Bodensee. Dort wird ein
vorzüglicher Blauer Spätburgunder angebaut, der
als Spezialität der dortigen Winzer gilt. Hier wie
auch in anderen Gegenden Badens stößt man immer wieder auch auf die großen Traubensorten der
Nachbarländer, zum Beispiel den Chardonnay, der
auf der Insel erfolgreich angebaut wird.

Baden – pampered by the sun

The situation in Baden, with its more favorable cli-
mate, is quite different. The region between Karlsruhe and Baden-Baden as far as the Kaiserstuhl in
the south is one of the warmest regions of Germany. Mostly white-wine grapes are grown here:
light ones like Müller-Thurgau and Silvaner; and
heavy ones like Ruländer. Riesling grapes grow
here too. Also popular are Weissherbst wines,
slightly sparkling rosés. The red wines in this region are mostly Spätburgunder or Schwarzriesling.
Baden is also the cradle of Germany's ecological
movement. Correspondingly, the principles of or-
ganic farming have been widely adopted here. The
Baden wine-growing region also includes the island
of Reichenau on Lake Constance. An excellent
Pinot Noir, a blue Spätburgunder, is grown there; it
is considered to be one of the local wine-growers'
specialities. Here, as in other areas of Baden, you
will also come across the great grape varieties from
neighboring countries, including the Chardonnay.

*Links: Luftbild vom Kaiserstuhl, typisch
ist die schachbrettartige Anordnung
der Weinparzellen. Rechts: Blick auf
Burkheim, Kaiserstuhl.*

*Left: Aerial picture of the Kaiserstuhl
with the typical chessboard arrangement
of vineyards. Right: View of Burkheim,
Kaiserstuhl.*

Calw, Baiersbronn, Freudenstadt und Rottweil

Calw, Baiersbronn, Freudenstadt and Rottweil

*Oberer Markt-
platz mit Rathaus
in Freudenstadt,
Schwarzwald.*

*The Upper Mar-
ket Place with
the Town Hall in
Freudenstadt, Black
Forest.*

Etwa 18 Kilometer südlich von Pforzheim liegt Calw, die Geburtsstadt Hermann Hesses, Autor von „Der Steppenwolf" und Literaturnobelpreisträger von 1946. Calw taucht in seinem Werk immer wieder als der fiktive Ort Gerbersau auf. Am Marktplatz steht sein Geburtshaus, nicht weit davon entfernt das Hermann-Hesse-Museum. Eine Besonderheit von Calw ist die um 1400 erbaute kleine gotische Brückenkapelle St. Nikolaus auf der Nikolausbrücke über die Nagold. Südwestlich von Calw zieht die Schwarzwaldgemeinde Baiersbronn eine spezielle Art von Pilgern an: Sie ist neben Bergisch-Gladbach die einzige deutsche Stadt, in der sich gleich zwei Restaurants mit drei Michelin-Sternen schmücken dürfen: das Restaurant Bareiss und die Schwarzwaldstube. Südlich des Gourmetdorfs gelangt man nach Freudenstadt, eine 1599 auf Veranlassung von Herzog Friedrich I. von

Württemberg erbaute Siedlung für die Arbeizter in den nahe gelegenen Silberbergwerken. Der quadratische Grundriss macht den Reißbrettcharakter deutlich. Wahrzeichen ist der Marktplatz mit den umlaufenden Laubengängen.

About 18 kilometers (11 miles) south of Pforzheim you will reach Calw, the birthplace of Hermann Hesse, the author of Steppenwolf and the winner of the Nobel Prize for Literature in 1946. Calw appears repeatedly in his works as the fictional town of Gerbersau. The house in which he was born stands on the market place, not far from the Hermann Hesse Museum. One of the most important landmarks in Calw is the little Gothic bridge chapel of St. Nicholas, built in 1400, which stands on the Nikolausbrücke across the Nagold. Southwest of Calw lies the Black Forest community of Baiersbronn, which attracts a special type of pilgrim. Apart from Bergisch-Gladbach it is the only town in Germany which can claim two restaurants with three Michelin stars: Restaurant Bareiss and the Schwarzwaldstube. South of the gourmet village you will arrive in Freudenstadt, a settlement established in 1599 following a decree by Duke Friedrich I of Württemberg for the workers employed in the nearby silver mines. The square plan draws attention to the checkerboard layout. The town's main landmark is the market place with its surrounding arcades.

Maskierte Narren prägen an Fasnet das Stadtbild in Rottweil.

Masked revelers fill the streets in Rottweil during the pre-Lenten Fasnet carnival.

Dort wo sich Schwarzwald und Schwäbische Alb berühren befindet sich die älteste Stadt Baden-Württembergs: Rottweil, 73 n. Chr. von den Römern gegründet. Mitte des 3. Jahrhunderts, als die Alemannen die Herrschaft übernahmen, ging die Siedlung allerdings unter. In der Stauferzeit, um 1200, wurde sie neu errichtet und 1268 in den Rang einer Reichsstadt erhoben. Der spätmittelalterliche Kern mit den erkergeschmückten Bürgerhäusern ist erhalten geblieben. Rottweil ist heute auch bekannt für die gleichnamige deutsche Hunderasse – ein Denkmal vor dem Stadtmuseum ist dem imposanten Vierbeiner gewidmet. Rottweiler werden gern als Wachhunde oder von der Polizei eingesetzt. Ein Besuchermagnet wird die Stadt alljährlich anlässlich der schwäbisch-alemannischen Fasnet. Den traditionellen Narrensprung durch das Schwarze Tor, das Wahrzeichen der Stadt, vollführen bis zu 3000 maskierte und verkleidete Narren, die in zahlreichen Zünften organisiert sind. Typische Figuren sind Teufel, Hexen und Tiergestalten, der Zug wird lautstark durch Rätschen und – für Rottweil typisch – Peitschenschläge begleitet.

At the intersection of Black Forest and the Swabian Alb lies Rottweil, the oldest town in Baden-Württemberg. It was founded in 73 A.D. by the Romans. In the middle of the third century, when the Alemannii conquered the region, the settlement was destroyed. Under the Hohenstaufens, in around 1200, it was rebuilt and in 1268 was elevated to the rank of an Imperial city. The late medieval town center with its burghers' houses adorned with oriel windows has survived. Rottweil is famous today for the German breed of dog which bears its name; a monument in front of the Municipal Museum is dedicated to this imposing creatures. Rottweilers are often used as guard dogs or by the police. The town attracts large numbers of visitors every year when the Swabian-Alemannic Fasnet carnival is celebrated. Up to 3000 masked and costumed revelers, arranged in various guilds, perform the traditional Fool's Leap through the Schwarzes Tor, the town's landmark gateway. Typical characters include devils, witches and animals, and the procession is accompanied by loud rattles and – typical of Rottweil – the cracking of whips.

Villingen-Schwenningen, Donaueschingen, Titisee

Villingen-Schwenningen, Donaueschingen, Titisee

Villingen-Schwenningen zählt ebenfalls zu den Hochburgen der schwäbisch-alemannischen Fasnet. Die Doppelstadt am Ostrand des Schwarzwalds entstand 1972 durch den Zusammenschluss des badischen Villingen mit dem württembergischen Schwenningen. Beide Städte sind frühmittelalterliche Gründungen. Im 16. Jahrhundert soll in Villingen ein Mann namens Romäus gelebt haben, der so groß war, dass er durch die Fenster der zweiten Stockwerke schauen konnte. Eine Reihe von Sagen ranken sich um diesen Riesen, zum Beispiel soll er ein Fuhrwerk, das seinen zwei Ochsen zu schwer geworden war, einfach mitsamt der Tiere auf den Schultern nach Hause getragen haben. Weiter südlich befindet sich in Donaueschingen die Quelle des zweitlängsten Flusses Europas. Unscheinbar sieht er aus, der Ursprung der Donau am Zusammenfluss von Brigach und Breg. Gut 2800 Kilometer weiter östlich, nachdem sie das Wasser vieler Nebenflüsse aufgenommen hat, wird die Donau ins Schwarze Meer münden. Einmal im Jahr sind in der Stadt besonders ungewöhnliche Töne zu hören: Im Oktober werden während der Donaueschinger Musiktage Kompositionen zeitgenössischer Musik erstaufgeführt. Erholung pur gibt es etwas weiter westlich, am Titisee mit dem Kurort Titisee-Neustadt. Nur noch 13 Kilometer sind es von hier aus bis zum 1493 Meter hohen Feldberg, der höchsten Erhebung des Schwarzwalds.

Villingen-Schwenningen is another stronghold of the Swabian-Alemannic Fasnet. The twin town on the eastern edge of the Black Forest was formed in 1972 by the amalgamation of Villingen, in Baden, with Schwenningen, in Württemberg. Both towns were originally founded during the early Middle Ages. During the 16th century it is claimed that a man named Romäus lived in Villingen; he was so tall that he could look out through the windows on the second floor. A number of legends surround the giant. He supposedly picked up a cart which was too heavy for his two oxen, together with the oxen, and carried it all home. Further south, in Donaueschingen, you will find the source of the second-longest river in Europe. The origin of the Danube at the confluence of the Brigach and Breg, looks unremarkable. More than 2800 kilometers (1750 miles) further east, after gathering up the water of numerous tributaries, the Danube flows into the Black Sea. Once a year you will hear very unusual sounds in the town. Contemporary musical compositions are premiered here in October during the Donaueschingen Music Festival. Things are somewhat quieter further to the west: Lake Titisee and the health resort of Titisee-Neustadt welcome guests for rest and recreation. From here it is only another 13 kilometers (8 miles) to the Feldberg, at 1493 meters (4897 feet) the highest mountain in the Black Forest.

Die Donauquelle in Donaueschingen: Mutter Baar – so heißt die Hochebene zwischen Schwarzwald und Schwäbischer Alb – weist der Donau den Weg nach Osten.

The source of the Danube in Donaueschingen: Mutter Baar – as the area of highland between the Black Forest and the Swabian Alb is known – shows the Danube its route westwards.

Kaiserstuhl – Weinbau auf dem Vulkan

Kaiserstuhl – viticulture on the volcano

Typisch für den Kaiserstuhl: Weinanbau in Terrassen. Altstadt von Vogtsburg-Burkheim, Kaiserstuhl.

Typical of the Kaiserstuhl: terraced vineyards. The historic town center of Vogtsburg-Burkheim on the Kaiserstuhl.

Der Kaiserstuhl im äußersten Südwesten Baden-Württembergs zählt zu den wärmsten Regionen Deutschlands – ideale Bedingungen für den Weinbau. Geologisch handelt es sich, mit Ausnahme des östlichen Drittels, um ein ehemaliges Vulkangebiet, die letzten Ausbrüche fanden vor etwa 19 Millionen Jahren statt. Über einen Zeitraum von zwei bis drei Millionen Jahren ist durch Ablagerungen und Auswehung die äußerst fruchtbare Lössschicht entstanden, auf der der Wein und sogar mediterrane Pflanzen hervorragend gedeihen. Hauptorte sind Vogtsburg, ein Zusammenschluss von sieben Gemeinden, Ihringen und Sasbach.

Lying in the far southwest of Baden-Württemberg, the Kaiserstuhl is one of the warmest regions in Germany, thereby providing ideal conditions for wine-growing. Geologically speaking, apart from the eastern third, this is a region which was formerly volcanic; the last eruptions took place some 19 million years ago. During the last two to three million years deposits and erosion have created the fertile loess layer on which the vines and other almost Mediterranean plants flourish. The main towns are Vogtsburg, an amalgamation of seven villages, Ihringen and Sasbach.

Freiburg – Stadt der Zähringer

Freiburg – The seat of the Dukes of Zähringen

Mit den Staufern verwandt war das schwäbische Fürstengeschlecht der Zähringer, das im 12. Jahrhundert eine bedeutende Machtstellung innehatte. Finanzielle Basis dieser Macht war der Silberbergbau im Schwarzwald. Neben Offenburg und Villingen ist auch Freiburg i. Br. eine Gründung der Zähringer. Auf dem heutigen Schlossberg ließ Herzog Bertold II. Ende des 11. Jahrhunderts eine Burg errichten; die Siedlung, die sich um die Burg bildete, erhielt 1120 Markt- und Stadtrechte. Anfang des 13. Jahrhunderts starb diese Fürstenlinie aus, den Freiburger Besitz erbten die Grafen von Freiburg. Die Bürger waren offenbar nicht zufrieden mit ihrer Herrschaft – wegen der Finanzen gab es häufig Streit –, sie kauften sich nach 150 Jahren frei und schlossen sich den Habsburgern an. Mit dem französischen Kaiser Napoleon endete Anfang des 19. Jahrhunderts die österreichische Zeit: Freiburg wurde badisch. Bereits 1457 erfolgte die Gründung der Albert-Ludwigs-Universität, die heute zu den besten Universitäten des Landes zählt. Als Tor zum Schwarzwald ist die Stadt ein beliebtes Touristenziel.

The Swabian princely family of the Dukes of Zähringen was related to the Hohenstaufens. They occupied a powerful position during the 12th century. The financial basis of their power was the silver mining in the Black Forest. Like Offenburg and Villingen Freiburg im Breisgau was also founded by them. Duke Bertold II had a fortress built on what is now the Castle Hill at the end of the eleventh century; the settlement which formed around the castle was awarded market and municipal rights in 1120. The princely line died out in the early thirteenth century, and their Freiburg property was inherited by the Counts of Freiburg. The citizens were evidently not satisfied with their rulers – there were frequent quarrels regarding finances –, and after 150 years they purchased their freedom and entered into an alliance with the Habsburgs. The Austrian era came to an end in the early nineteenth century under Napoleon: Freiburg became part of Baden. The Albert Ludwig University was founded in 1457; today it is one of the top universities in the country. As the gateway to the Black Forest the town is a popular tourist destination to this day.

Das Münster ist das Wahrzeichen von Freiburg und bildet ihr Zentrum. Der gotische Kirchturm erreicht eine Höhe von 116 Metern und ist einer der wenigen Kirchtürme, der bereits um 1330, also noch im Mittelalter, vollendet wurde. Bedeutsam in der Innenausstattung ist der Hochaltar von Hans Baldung Grien sowie ein Altar, den Hans Holbein der Jüngere gestaltet hat. Auf dem Marktplatz um das Münster herum findet regelmäßig ein Wochenmarkt statt. Cafés und Restaurants laden zum

Das Schwabentor ist eines der beiden Stadttore von Freiburg. In unmittelbarer Nähe befindet sich das Gasthaus „Zum roten Bären" – das den Anspruch erhebt, das älteste Gasthaus Deutschlands zu sein.

The Schwabentor is one of the two city gates of Freiburg. Nearby you will find the inn "Zum roten Bären" (The Red Bear), which claims to be the oldest in Germany.

Verweilen ein. Dem Besucher werden die berühmten „Bächle" auffallen, kleine Wasserrinnen an den Rändern der Gassen und Straßen der Fußgängerzone. Es kommt nicht selten vor, dass man versehentlich in sie hineintritt und nasse Füße bekommt – ob das aber dann auf eine spätere Heirat mit einem Freiburger oder einer Freiburgerin deutet, wie eine badische Sage berichtet, sei dahingestellt. Nicht versäumen sollten Besucher die beiden Stadttore, das Martins- und das Schwabentor, und einen Spaziergang auf den Schlossberg. Das älteste Gasthaus soll es hier ebenfalls geben – „Zum roten Bären" heißt es und befindet sich ganz in der Nähe des Schwabentors. Es wird erstmals 1120 erwähnt.

The Münster (Cathedral) is the town's main landmark and focal point. The Gothic church tower soars to a height of 116 meters (380 feet) and is one of the few church towers which was completed during the Middle Ages, in 1330. The interior is important because of the High Altar by Hans Baldung Grien as well as another altar designed by Hans Holbein the Younger. A weekly market is held regularly on the market place surrounding the cathedral. Cafés and restaurants invite visitors to tarry awhile. They will certainly notice the famous "Bächle", the streams running in open gullies along the edges of the alleys and streets in the pedestrian area. Many a visitor has stepped into one accidentally – it is not certain, however, whether that really means that you will one day marry a citizen of Freiburg, as a local legend maintains. Do not miss the two city gates, the Martinstor and the Schwabentor; and make sure you leave time for a walk on the Castle Hill. It is said that you will also find the oldest inn here: "Zum roten Bären" (The Red Bear) lies not far from the Schwabentor. It was first mentioned in records in 1120.

Eingang des Hauses zum Walfisch (1514–1516) in der Franziskanergasse, Freiburg i. Br., hinter der Martinskirche. Hier wohnte einst auch der Humanist Erasmus von Rotterdam.

The entrance of the Haus zum Walfisch (1514-1516) behind St. Martin's Church in Franziskanergasse, Freiburg im Breisgau. The humanist Erasmus von Rotterdam once lived here.

Der Norden – von der Kurpfalz zum Taubertal

The North – from the Electoral Palatinate to the Tauber Valley

Dort, wo Baden-Württemberg an Rhein-land-Pfalz, Hessen und Bayern grenzt, sind die Übergänge zu den Nachbarn unmerklich. Mannheim und Ludwigs-hafen trennt nur der Rhein, von Wert-heim ist es nicht mehr weit nach Würz-burg. Das romantische Heidelberg liegt hier, die Stadt, die wie kaum eine andere im Ausland mit Deutschland in Verbin-dung gebracht wird – eines der ersten Ziele der zahllosen Touristen.

At the point where Baden-Württemberg borders on Rhineland-Palatinate, Hesse and Bavaria, the boundaries to the neighboring regions are fluid. Mann-heim and Ludwigshafen are separated only be the Rhine, and from Wertheim it is not far to Würzburg. Romantic Heidelberg lies here, the town which is regarded perhaps more than any oth-er as the very epitome of Germany by visitors from abroad, and which is there-fore one of the main goals of countless tourists.

Heidelberg, kurpfälzische Residenz am Neckar

Heidelberg, royal capital of the Electoral Palatinate

In dieser Stadt kann man „sein Herz verlieren", so klang es schon 1925 in einem Schlager, mit dem der österreichische Operettenkomponist Fred Raymond die Neckarstadt verewigte. Wenn japanische oder amerikanische Touristen Deutschland besuchen, dann steht Heidelberg ganz oben auf ihrer Liste. Zu Recht: Die Altstadt, im Zweiten Weltkrieg weitgehend verschont, ist hervorragend erhalten und heute Fußgängerzone. Berühmt und nicht zu übersehen ist das Heidelberger Schloss auf dem Königsstuhl über dem Neckar, die wohl bekannteste Burgruine Deutschlands (erreichbar zu Fuß, aber auch mit der Heidelberger Bergbahn, eine historische Standseilbahn). Das mehrfach erweiterte und umgebaute Schloss wurde 1693 im Pfälzischen Erbfolgekrieg von französischen Truppen zerstört. Wiederaufbauversuche scheiterten am Geld. Lange Zeit wurden die Reste des Renaissancebaus als Steinbruch genutzt, erst im 19. Jahrhundert, in der Romantik, rückte die Schönheit der Ruine in den Blick. Wesentlich dazu beigetragen haben einige berühmte Touristen: Victor Hugo, William Turner und Mark Twain.

A popular song of 1925 claimed that you can "lose your heart" in Heidelberg. Austrian composer of operettas Fred Raymond immortalized the town on the Neckar. Whenever American or Japanese tourists visit Germany, Heidelberg is always very near the top of their list. And rightfully so. The Old Town, virtually undamaged during World War II, has been immaculately preserved and is a pedestrian area today. Equally famous and impossible to miss is Heidelberg Castle, perched on the Königsstuhl above the Neckar and the most famous ruin in Germany (accessible on foot, or alternatively via the Heidelberger Bergbahn, a historic funicular railway). Rebuilt and extended on several occasions, the castle was destroyed in 1693 by French troops during the Palatinate War of Succession. Attempts at restoration have failed because of the costs involved. For a long time the remains of the Renaissance building were used as a stone quarry; only in the nineteenth century, during the Romantic Age, was the ruin seen in a different light. Some of the famous tourists of the age contributed to the change of attitude: Victor Hugo, J.M.W. Turner and Mark Twain.

Heidelberg ist geprägt durch die Universität, die bereits 1386 gegründet wurde. Die Hochschulen sind heute der größte Arbeitgeber der Stadt. Schon früh hatte sich Heidelberg der Reformation angeschlossen. Kurfürst Ottheinrich (1556–1559) schaffte den Lehrstuhl für katholische Theologie ab. Der fast 200 Kilogramm schwere Regent lebte verschwenderisch und starb kinderlos. Die erste Blütezeit Heidelbergs dauerte bis ins 18. Jahrhundert. Damals regierte

Seite 70, 71: Marktplatz von Bad Mergentheim mit den Zwillingshäusern. Stadtturm und Burg, Wertheim. Blick auf Schwäbisch Hall. Altstadt in Creglingen. Stadttor am Schlosspark des Deutschordensschlosses, Bad Mergentheim.

Page 70, 71: The market square and the "Twin Houses" in Bad Mergentheim. The Stadtturm tower and the castle in Wertheim. View of Schwäbisch Hall. The historic town center of Creglingen. The gateway leading to the castle park of Teutonic Knights' Castle, Bad Mergentheim.

Blick vom Philosophenweg aus auf die Altstadt mit Schloss, Heilig-Geist-Kirche und Alte Brücke.
View from the Philosophers' Walk across the Old Town with the Castle, the Church of the Holy Ghost and the Old Bridge.

Kurfürst Karl III. Philipp (1716–1742). Eine schillernde Figur an dessen Hof war der Hofzwerg Perkeo, den der Fürst aus Südtirol als Kuriosität mitgebracht hatte. Zu seinem Namen kam der wohl kluge Mann, weil er auf die Frage, ob er noch Wein trinken möchte, auf Italienisch mit „perché no?" („Warum nicht?") geantwortet haben soll. Perkeo machte Karriere: Er wurde Mundschenk und Hüter des Heidelberger Fasses, zu seiner Zeit mit 195 000 Litern Inhalt das größte der Welt. Man erzählt sich, dass Perkeo von Kindesbeinen an nur Wein getrunken habe und erst als über 80-jähriger erstmals krank wurde. Der Arzt habe ihm damals geraten, nur noch Wasser zu trinken, worauf er tags darauf starb.

Heidelberg's character is determined by its university, founded as long ago as 1386. Today these institutes of learning are the town's most important employer. Heidelberg supported the Reformation from an early phase. Elector Ottheinrich (1556-1559), abolished the chair of Catholic Theology. The ruler, who weighed almost 200 kilograms, lived extravagantly and died childless. Heidelberg's first golden age lasted into the 18th century. The ruler at that time was Elector Karl III Philipp (1716-1742). One of the most flamboyant characters at his court was the dwarf Perkeo, whom the prince had brought with him from South Tyrol as a curiosity. He was highly intelligent, and his name came from the fact that when he was asked if he would like any more wine, he answered in Italian by saying "perché no?" ("Why not?"). Perkeo had a distinguished career. He became cup-bearer and was the guardian of the Great Vat, which had a capacity of 195,000 liters (51,480 gallons). It is said that he drank nothing but wine from childhood onwards and that he became ill for the very first time when he was over 80 years old. The doctor advised him to drink nothing but water, and he died.

Das im Neo-renaissancestil erbaute Rathaus in Heidelberg, davor ein Straßencafé.

Street café by the neo-renaissance Town Hall in Heidelberg.

Planstadt *Mannheim,* Schwetzingen, Weinheim

The planned city of Mannheim, Schwetzingen, Weinheim

Die Geburtsstunde von Mannheim schlug 1720. Kurpfälzische Residenz war zu dieser Zeit Heidelberg, bis der katholische Kurfürst Karl Philipp (1716–1742) beim Versuch, die Heiliggeist-Kirche zur katholischen Hofkirche umzuwidmen, am protestantischen Widerstand scheiterte. Verärgert kehrte er darauf Heidelberg den Rücken und verlegte die kurpfälzische Residenz nach Mannheim. Im selben Jahr wurde auch mit dem Bau des Schlosses begonnen. Das gitterförmige Straßennetz geht noch zurück auf Kurfürst Friedrich IV. (um 1600). Mit der Verlegung der Residenz begann eine erste Blütezeit der Stadt, die bis zum Ende des 18. Jahrhunderts dauerte. Der kurpfälzische Hof erwies sich als Förderer von Musik, Kunst und Wissenschaft. Schillers „Die Räuber" kamen 1782 in Mannheim zur Uraufführung, sehr zum Ärger des württembergischen Herzogs Karl Eugen, der den Dichter 14

Tage ins Gefängnis sperrte und ihm untersagte, weiterhin „dergleichen Zeugs" zu schreiben. Um 1750 wurde die Mannheimer Schule, eine Komponistenschule der Vorklassik um Johann Anton Stamitz (1717–1757) gegründet – Kurfürst war damals Karl IV.

Mannheim was founded in 1720. Heidelberg was the residential capital of the Palatine Electors until the Catholic Elector Karl Philipp (1716-1742) attempted to re-dedicate the Holy Ghost Church as a Catholic court church but failed as a result of the Protestant opposition. He was so annoyed that he abandoned Heidelberg and moved the residential capital to Mannheim. Construction of the palace began during the same year. The checkerboard street network was the work of Elector Friedrich IV (c. 1600). The relocation of the Residence marked the start of the town's first golden age, which lasted until the end of the 18th century. The court of the Electors Palatine patronized music, art and science. Friedrich Schiller's "The Robbers" had its première in 1782 in the theater in Mannheim, much to the annoyance of Duke Karl Eugen of Württemberg, who locked the writer up in prison for fourteen days and forbade him to continue to write "things like that." In around 1750 the Mannheim School, an important pre-classical group of composers, was founded around Johann Anton Stamitz (1717-1757).

Der Wasserturm mit Springbrunnen und Park auf dem Friedrichsplatz in Mannheim.

The water tower with fountain and park at Friedrichsplatz in Mannheim.

Die Heidelberger Schlossruine diente unter anderem als Steinbruch für den Bau des Schwetzinger Schlosses, das 1720 einige Zeit für den Kurfürsten Karl Philipp nach seinem Auszug aus Heidelberg als Ausweichquartier diente. 1742 wurde es als Sommerresidenz im Barockstil ausgebaut, 1752 eröffnete das Schlosstheater. Unter dem Kurfürsten Karl Theodor diente die Residenz auch als Jagdschloss. Damals wurde der typische Barockgarten zu einem Garten im offeneren englischen Stil erweitert. Heute ist Schwetzingen mit seinem Rokokotheater alljährlich Schauplatz der gleichnamigen Festspiele. Neben Konzerten kamen seit 1952 hier zahlreiche Bühnenwerke zur Uraufführung, darunter viele der Stücke des Komponisten Hans Werner Henze. Schwetzingen ist heute im Übrigen auch für seinen hervorragenden Spargel überregional bekannt. Weinheim liegt etwa 18 Kilometer nördlich von Heidelberg. Die auf dem Schlossberg der Stadt erbaute Burg Windeck (um 1130) diente dem Schutz der Besitzungen des Klosters Lorsch und wurde im 17. Jahrhundert von den Franzosen zerstört; sie ist heute eine Ruine und ein beliebtes Ausflugsziel.

The ruins of Heidelberg Castle served, among other things, as the stone quarry for the construction of Schwetzingen Palace, which in 1720 served Elector Karl Philipp as a temporary residence after he had abandoned

Das Schloss von Weinheim ist heute Rathaus und Sitz der Stadtverwaltung.

Weinheim Palace is now the Town Hall and the seat of the municipal administration.

Heidelberg. It was extended and transformed into a summer residence in the Baroque style in 1742; in 1752 the palace theater was inaugurated. Under Elector Karl Theodor it also served as a hunting palace. At that time, too, the typical Baroque garden was extended to form a park in the less formal English style. Today, Schwetzingen and its Rococo theater provide the setting for an annual festival. Apart from concerts, since 1952 numerous staged works have had their première here, including a number of works by the composer Hans Werner Henze. Incidentally, Schwetzingen is also famous today for its excellent asparagus. Weinheim lies some 18 kilometers (11 miles) north of Heidelberg. Windeck Castle, built in around 1130 on the castle Hill above the town served to protect the property of Lorsch Monastery. It was destroyed by the French during the 17th century and remains a ruin today. It is a popular excursion destination.

SPECIAL | Naturparks in Baden-Württemberg

Nature Parks in Baden-Württemberg

Naturerlebnis und Erholung

In Baden-Württemberg gibt es sieben Naturparks, das sind großräumige Areale, in denen Natur- und Landschaftsschutz eine entscheidende Rolle spielen. Etwa 29 Pozent der Landesfläche nehmen diese Naherholungsgebiete ein. Von Nord nach Süd:

❶ Naturpark Neckartal-Odenwald (1292 km²). Der Park erstreckt sich von Weinheim und Heidelberg im Westen bis Hardheim im Osten. Höhepunkte sind neben Heidelberg und Weinheim selbst Zwingenberg mit seiner Burg und der Wolfsschlucht sowie die Eberstädter Tropfsteinhöhle.

❷ Naturpark Stromberg-Heuchelberg (328 km²). Bei dem zwischen Bretten im Westen und Besigheim im Osten gelegenen Park sind beliebte Ziele der nordwestlich von Besigheim gelegene Michaelsberg, das Wahrzeichen des Zabergäus, und natürlich die UNESCO-Welterbestätte Maulbronn.

❸ Naturpark Schwäbisch-Fränkischer Wald (904 km²). Der Park liegt nordöstlich von Stuttgart zwischen den Flüssen Neckar im Westen, Kocher im Osten und Norden sowie Rems im Süden. Höhepunkt sind der Obergermanisch-Rätische Limes bei Grab und Welzheim sowie das Kloster Lorch.

❹ Naturpark Schwarzwald Mitte/Nord (3600 km²). Der größte Naturpark Deutschlands befindet sich zwischen Karlsruhe und Pforzheim im Norden und Lahr sowie Schramberg im Süden. Naturhöhepunkte sind hier das Wildseemoor östlich von Baden-Baden, der Mummelsee bei der Hornisgrinde (1163 m) und das Gottschlägtal mit seinen Wasserfällen nördlich von Offenburg.

❺ Naturpark Schönbuch (256 km²). Nördlich von Tübingen liegt dieser kleinste und zugleich älteste Naturpark des Landes. Höhepunkte sind die Klosteranlage Bebenhausen und die Domäne Einsiedel.

❻ Naturpark Südschwarzwald (3215 km²). Von Sankt Georgen im Norden bis Lörrach und Bad Säckingen im Süden erstreckt sich dieser an Höhepunkten besonders reiche Park. Der höchste Berg des Schwarzwalds, der Feldberg (1493 m), aber auch Aussichtsberge wie der Kandel (1242 m) und der Belchen (1414 m) befinden sich hier. Titi- und Schluchsee laden ein, die Wutachschlucht und die Triberger Wasserfälle sind begehrte Wanderziele.

❼ Naturpark Obere Donau (857 km²). Zwischen Schwarzwald im Westen und Allgäu im Osten auf der Hochfläche der Schwäbischen Alb. Höhepunkte sind hier die Donauversickerung bei Möhringen, das Freilichtmuseum Neuhausen ob Eck bei Tuttlingen sowie das Kloster Beuron.

Nature experience and recreation

There are seven nature parks in Baden-Württemberg. These recreational areas cover some 29 percent of the total land area. From north to south:

❶ Naturpark Neckartal-Odenwald (1292 km²/ 492 sq. mi.). The park extends from Weinheim and Heidelberg in the west to Hardheim in the east. Apart from the towns of Heidelberg and Weinheim the highlights include Zwingenberg and its castle, the Wolfsschlucht and the caves at Eberstadt.

❷ Naturpark Stromberg-Heuchelberg (328 km²/ 125 sq. mi.). The park lies between Bretten in the west and Besigheim in the east. Popular destinations are the Michaelsberg northwest of Besigheim, the landmark of the Zabergäu, and the UNESCO World Heritage site of Maulbronn.

❸ Naturpark Schwäbisch-Fränkischer Wald (904 km²/ 344 sq. mi.). The park lies northeast of Stuttgart between the rivers Neckar in the west, Kocher

Das Eyachtal im Naturpark Nordschwarzwald, die Eyach ist ein linker Nebenfluss der Enz, einem Nebenfluss des Neckar.

The Eyach valley in the North Black Forest Nature Park. The Eyach is a tributary on the left-hand bank of the Enz, which in turn flows into the Neckar.

in the east and north and Rems in the south. The highlights here are the Upper Germanic-Raetian Limes near Grab and Welzheim and Lorch Monastery.

❹ Naturpark Schwarzwald Mitte/Nord (3600 km²/ 1372 sq. mi.) Germany's largest nature park lies between Karlsruhe and Pforzheim in the north and Lahr and Schramberg in the south. The natural highlights here are the Wildsee moor landscape east of Baden-Baden; Lake Mummelsee near the Hornisgrinde (1163 m/ 3815 ft), and the waterfalls of the Gottschläg Valley north of Offenburg.

❺ Naturpark Schönbuch (156 km²/ 59 sq. mi.). The smallest and oldest nature park in Baden-Württemberg lies north of Tübingen. The highlights are the monastery complex at Bebenhausen and Einsiedel Domain.

❻ Naturpark Südschwarzwald (3215 km²/ 1241 sq. mi.). This park, which includes a large number of high spots, extends from Sankt Georgen in the north to Lörrach and Bad Säckingen in the south. The highest mountain in the Black Forest, the Feldberg (1493 m/ 4897 ft), and mountains with spectacular views like the Kandel (1242 m/ 4074 ft) and the Belchen (1414 m/ 4638 ft) will be found here. Lakes Titisee and Schluchsee invite visitors, and the Wutach gorge and the Triberg waterfalls are popular hiking destinations.

❼ Naturpark Obere Donau (857 km²/ 327 sq. mi.). The nature park lies north of Lake Constance on the elevated stretch of the Swabian Alp between the Black Forest in the west and the Allgäu in the east. The highlights here are the Donauversickerung (Danube Sink) near Möhringen, the open-air museum in Neuhausen ob Eck near Tuttlingen and Beuron Monastery.

① Neckartal-Odenwald
② Stromberg-Heuchelberg
③ Schwäbisch-Fränkischer Wald
④ Schwarzwald Mitte/Nord
⑤ Schönbuch
⑥ Südschwarzwald
⑦ Obere Donau

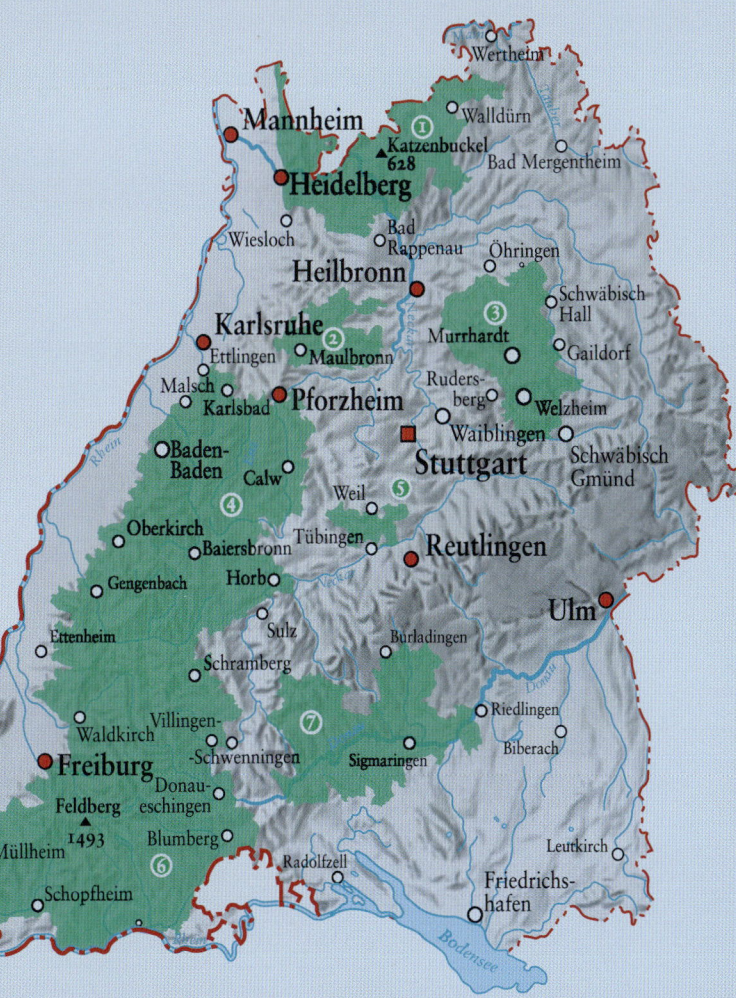

Eberbach, Mosbach, Schloss Zwingenberg

Eberbach, Mosbach, Zwingenberg Castle

Das Palm'sche Haus in Mosbach, Pulverturm (15. Jahrhundert) in Eberbach.

The Palmsches Haus in Mosbach; the Powder Tower (15th century) in Eberbach.

Im Naturpark Neckartal-Odenwald liegt Eberbach. Vier Türme, Reste der mittelalterlichen Befestigung, ragen markant über die Altstadt. Im Stadtwald steht einer der höchsten Bäume Deutschlands, eine über 62 Meter hohe, etwa 110-jährige Douglasie. Zwingenberg ist durch sein Schloss und die alljährlich hier stattfindenden Freilichtspiele überregional bekannt. Carl Maria von Webers romantische Oper „Der Freischütz" steht dabei im Mittelpunkt. Die in der Nähe liegende Wolfsschlucht hatte den Komponisten zu seinem Werk inspiriert. Die Kreisstadt Mosbach lohnt sich allein schon wegen des Palm'schen Hauses am Markt (1610) mit reich geschmücktem Fachwerk im fränkischen Stil.

Eberbach lies in the Neckar Valley-Odenwald nature park. Four medieval towers rise impressively above the old town. In the Stadtwald you can see one of the tallest trees in Germany, a Douglas fir which is over 62 meters (203 feet) high and 110 years old. Zwingenberg is famous beyond the state boundaries for its castle and the annual open-air festival which is held there. The highlight is a production of Carl Maria von Weber's romantic opera Der Freischütz. The Wolfsschlucht gorge in the vicinity inspired the composer to write the work. The district town of Mosbach is worth visiting just to see the Palmsches Haus on the market place (1610) with its richly decorated timber façade.

Maulbronn – Kloster, Schule, Weltkulturerbe

Maulbronn – monastery, school, World Cultural Heritage

Der Zisterzienserorden wirkte hinter diesen Klostermauern vom 12. bis zum 16. Jahrhundert. 1993 wurde die nahezu vollständig erhaltene Anlage als Weltkulturerbe von der UNESCO anerkannt. Nach seiner Gründung in der Mitte des 12. Jahrhunderts entwickelte sich das Kloster bald zu einem wirtschaftlichen und politischen Zentrum der Gegend. Den Maulbronner Mönchen wird die Erfindung der Maultasche zugeschrieben. Die mit Fleischbrät gefüllten Teigtaschen soll sich ein gewiefter Ordensbruder ausgedacht haben, damit Gott nicht merkte, wenn die Mönche an Freitagen und in der Fastenzeit doch heimlich Fleisch verzehrten. Auch um den Klosterbrunnen rankt sich eine Legende: Die Quelle und damit den Standort des Klosters soll ein von Gott geleitetes Maultier entdeckt haben. Um diese Quelle wurde das Kloster erbaut. Die Klosterkirche ist im Stil der oberrheinischen Spätromanik ganz im Geist der Lehren des Bernhard von Clairvaux gestaltet: Die Reformbewegung der Zisterzienser bevorzugte schlichte, schmucklose Kirchen statt Prunkbauten – ohne Krypta, Empore und sogar ohne Turm. Seit 1556 befindet sich im Kloster eine evangelische Klosterschule, heute das Evangelische Seminar, ein staatliches Gymnasium mit Internat. Zu den berühmtesten Schülern gehörten Johannes Kepler, Friedrich Hölderlin und Hermann Hesse. Im Kloster finden regelmäßig Konzerte statt.

The Cistercian order lived and worked within these monastery walls between the twelfth and the sixteenth century. In 1993 the complex was added to the list of UNESCO World Cultural Heritage sites. The monastery was founded in the middle of the twelfth century and soon grew into one of the economic and political centers of the region. Legend has it that the monks of Maulbronn were responsible for inventing the Maultasche, a local pasta speciality. The ravioli-like pockets of dough, usually filled with meat, were supposedly invented by a clever member of the order, so that God would not notice if the monks secretly ate meat on Fridays during Lent. There is also a legend relating to the monastery well. It is maintained that the spring and hence the location of the monastery was discovered by a mule which was led by God. The monastery church is built in the late Romanesque style and is designed in the spirit of the doctrines of St Bernard of Clairvaux: the Cistercian reform movement preferred unadorned churches instead of magnificent buildings – without a crypt and gallery and without a tower. Since 1556 the monastery has housed a Protestant church school; today it is the Evangelisches Seminar, a state grammar school with a boarding section. Among its most famous pupils were Johannes Kepler, Friedrich Hölderlin and Hermann Hesse. Concerts are held at regular intervals in the monastery.

UNESCO-Welterbe seit 1993: das Zisterzienserkloster Maulbronn. Der Kreuzgang mit Brunnen, Fachwerkhäuser im Innenhof des Klosters.

A UNESCO World Heritage site since 1993: the Cistercian Abbey of Maulbronn. The cloister with fountain, timbered houses in the inner courtyard of the monastery.

Bad Mergentheim,
Tauberbischofsheim

Bad Mergentheim, Tauberbischofsheim

Der Deutsche Orden hatte zwischen 1526 und 1809 in Bad Mergentheim seinen Hauptsitz. Der imposante Komplex des Deutschordensschlosses führt heute als Museum durch die Geschichte des Ordens, der auf einen im 12. Jahrhundert in der Zeit der Kreuzzüge gegründeten Ritterorden zurückgeht. Das Schloss liegt außerhalb der Stadt, und ist von ihr durch einen Graben getrennt. Das deutet darauf hin, dass es ursprünglich eine mittelalterliche Wasserburg war. 18 Hochmeister – so werden im Deutschen Orden die Träger des höchsten Amtes bezeichnet – haben das Schloss genutzt und immer wieder für Um- und Anbauten gesorgt. Berühmt ist die von dem Renaissancebaumeister Blasius Berwart konstruierte Wendeltreppe (Ende 16. Jahrhundert). Bei der 1730 bis 1736 umgebauten Schlosskirche ist der Barockeinfluss unverkennbar.

Frühklassizistisch ist dagegen der Kapitelsaal (1778–1782). In der Stadt sehenswert sind auch der Marktplatz mit den Zwillingshäusern, dem Rathaus und dem Münster St. Baptist. 1826 wurde die erste von vier Heilquellen, die heutige Wilhelmsquelle, entdeckt.

Between 1526 and 1809 the Teutonic Knights had their headquarters in Bad Mergentheim. Today the imposing complex of the former castle of the Teutonic Order is a museum explaining the history of the order, which goes back to a chivalric order founded in the twelfth century during the time of the crusades. The castle is situated near the town but separated from the latter by a moat which indicates that the castle was a moated complex during the Middle Ages. Eighteen Grand Masters – as the holders of the highest office within the order are called – have used the castle and repeatedly renovated and extended it. Particularly famous is the spiral staircase built by Renaissance master builder Blasius Berwart during the late 16th century. The Baroque influence is much in evidence in the case of the castle church(1730-1736). The pillared hall, by contrast, is early neo-classical (1778-82). Worth seeing in the town itself is the market place with the famous Twin Houses, the Town Hall and the St. Baptist Minster. In 1826 the Wilhelmsquelle, the first of the town's healing springs was discovered (there are now four of them).

Brunnen im Kurpark der Deutschordensstadt Bad Mergentheim.

Fountain in the spa park in Bad Mergentheim, the home of the Teutonic Order.

Tauberbischofsheim im „lieblichen Taubertal" liegt – wie auch Bad Mergentheim – an der Romantischen Straße, die von Würzburg bis Füssen führt, eine der beliebtesten deutschen Ferienstraßen. Der Name der Stadt hat sich erst 1850 eingebürgert, zuvor hieß sie Bischofsheim. Gegen Ende des 13. Jahrhunderts wurde das kurmainzische Schloss (heute Landesmuseum) mit dem Türmersturm erbaut. 1806 kam die Stadt im Zuge der Säkularisierung zum neu gegründeten Großherzogtum Baden. Stadtpatronin ist die um 710 im englischen Wessex geborene heilige Lioba (deutsch: Truthgeb). Eine Legende umgibt die Geburt der Nonne: Ihre Mutter Ebba träumte, dass eine Kirchenglocke zu läuten anfing, sobald sie ihren Bauch berührte. Sie deutete dies als Zeichen für die Geburt Liobas, und beschloss, das Kind Christus zu weihen. Lioba wird deshalb meist mit einem Glöckchen dargestellt. Um 735 holte sie Bonifatius, mit dem Lioba verwandt war, ins damalige Fränkische Reich, wo sie als Missionarin wirkte und im Nonnenkloster von Tauberbischofsheim eine Klosterschule gründete.

Like Bad Mergentheim, Tauberbischofsheim in the "Lovely Tauber Valley" lies on the Romantic Road which leads from Würzburg to Füssen and which is one of the most popular holiday routes in Germany. The town's name only dates back to 1850; before that it was known as "Bischofsheim". The Kurmainzisches Schloss (today the state museum) with the Türmersturm was built towards the end of the thirteenth century. In 1806, during the secularization, the town was passed over to the newly founded Grand Duchy of Baden. The town's patron saint is St. Lioba, born in Wessex in England in around 710. There is a legend surrounding the nun's birth: her mother Ebba dreamt that a church bell began to ring whenever she touched her stomach. She interpreted this as a sign relating to Lioba's birth, and decided to dedicate the child to Christ. Lioba is therefore usually depicted with a little bell. In around 735 St. Boniface, who was related to Lioba, summoned her to the kingdom of the Franks, where she worked as a missionary and founded a convent school in the convent at Tauberbischofsheim.

Das kurmainzische Schloss in Tauberbischofsheim beherbergt heute das Landesmuseum.

The Electoral Palace in Tauberbischofsheim now houses the state museum.

Heilbronn, Wein- und Käthchenstadt

Heilbronn, the town of wine and "Käthchen"

Als Zentrum des Unterlands hat Heilbronn seit dem 13. Jahrhundert eine Tradition als Reichs- und Patrizierstadt. Das gotische Rathaus, 1417 errichtet, erhielt um 1580 eine Schmuckfassade mit einer astronomischen Uhr im Stil der Renaissance. Die dem heiligen Kilian geweihte Pfarrkirche geht auf einen Bau aus dem 12. Jahrhundert zurück und wurde im Laufe der Zeit mehrfach ergänzt und erweitert. Auf der Turmspitze befindet sich nicht wie üblich ein Kreuz, sondern ein Landsknecht als symbolischer Bannerträger der Stadt. Heilbronn nennt sich „Käthchenstadt", Heinrich von Kleist stand mit seinem Drama „Das Käthchen von Heilbronn" (1807–1808) Pate. Ob es ein Vorbild für die Hauptfigur des „historischen Ritterschauspiels", die uneheliche Tochter eines Kaisers, gegeben hat, ist umstritten. Im Käthchenhaus am Marktplatz, ein umgebautes Patrizierhaus aus dem 14. Jahrhundert, soll das „echte" Käthchen gelebt haben. Wie auch immer: Die Käthchenfigur gehört zu Heilbronn. Ein wesentlicher Wirtschaftsfaktor der Stadt ist der Weinbau: Nach Brackenheim und Lauffen verfügt die Stadt über die drittgrößte Rebfläche in Württemberg. Es wird überwiegend Rotwein angebaut. Lauffen am Neckar liegt etwa zehn Kilometer südlich von Heilbronn. Lauffen, die zweitgrößte Weinbaugemeinde Württembergs, ist der Geburtsort des Dichters Friedrich Hölderlin (1770–1843).

Heilbronn is the center of the lowlands and since the thirteenth century it has had a tradition as an Imperial and aristocratic city. The Gothic Town Hall, built in 1417, was given a decorative façade in around 1580 including a Renaissance-style astronomic clock. The parish church is dedicated to St. Kilian and goes back to a twelfth-century building. Across the centuries it was enlarged and extended several times. On the top of the tower, instead of a cross as usual, it has a countryman, the symbolic standard-bearer of the town. Heilbronn is also known as the "Käthchenstadt," a reference to Heinrich von Kleist and his drama Das Käthchen von Heilbronn (1807-1808). Opinions differ as to whether there was a real-life model for the main character in the "historic story of chivalry," the illegitimate daughter of an emperor. The girl on whom Käthchen is modeled is said to have lived in the Käthchenhaus on the market place, a patrician residence dating from the 14th century. Be that as it may: The figure of Käthchen is very much part of Heilbronn. Wine-growing is an important economic factor here: The town can claim the third-largest area of vineyards in Württemberg. Mostly red wine is grown. Lauffen on the Neckar, incidentally, lies about ten kilometers (6 miles) south of Heilbronn. The second-largest wine-growing town in Württemberg was the birthplace of the poet Friedrich Hölderlin (1770-1843).

Das beleuchtete Rathaus, das Käthchen-Denkmal und die Kilianskirche aus dem 12. Jahrhundert – das Wahrzeichen der Stadt Heilbronn – am Tag und in der Nacht angestrahlt.

The illuminated Town Hall, the Käthchen Memorial and the Church of St. Kilian, dating from the twelfth century – the main landmark of the town of Heilbronn – by day and illuminated at night.

Weinsberg, Wein und treue Weiber

Weinsberg, wine and "true women"

Die Burg der treuen Frauen: Weinsberg. Weinsberg liegt in einem Weinbaugebiet.

Weinsberg, the castle of the true women: Weinsberg lies in a wine-producing region.

Die „Burgruine Weibertreu" ist die Ruine einer vermutlich im 11. Jahrhundert erbauten Burg bei Weinsberg. Ihren Namen verdankt sie einer Begebenheit im Jahr 1140: Der Stauferkönig Konrad III. belagerte die Burg mehrere Wochen lang, bis sie sich am 21. Dezember ergeben musste. Die Frauen erhielten freien Abzug und durften mitnehmen, was sie auf ihren Schultern tragen konnten. Den Männern drohte der Tod. Daraufhin schulterten die Frauen ihre Männer und retten ihnen so das Leben, der König stand zu seinem Wort. 1525, während der Bauernkriege wurden Burg und Stadt geplündert und zerstört. Der Burgberg ist zugleich einer der Weinberge der Stadt.

The ruined castle of Weibertreu is the ruin of a fortress near Weinsberg which is thought to have been built during the eleventh century. It owes its name to an event in the year 1140: the Staufer king Konrad III besieged the castle for several weeks, until the inhabitants were forced to surrender. The women were allowed to leave and could take with them as much as they could carry. The men were threatened with death. Thereupon the women shouldered their husbands and thus saved their lives; the king kept his promise. In 1525, during the Peasant Wars, the castle and the town were both plundered and destroyed. The Castle Hill is also one of the town's vineyards.

Wertheim, Creglingen bis Schwäbisch Hall

Wertheim, Creglingen to Schwäbisch Hall

Am Zusammenfluss von Tauber und Main liegt das malerische altfränkische Städtchen Wertheim, das als „Klein Heidelberg" bezeichnet wird. Unter den vielen schönen Fachwerkhäusern der Stadt fällt das Haus der Ritter von Zobel (1520) am Marktplatz besonders auf. Es ist so schmal, dass die Bewohner darin wohl nur längs ihre Betten unterbringen konnten. Im Erdgeschoss befindet sich heute ein kleines Ladengeschäft. An der Stiftskirche und der spätgotischen Kilianskapelle vorbei führen Stufen hinauf zur eindrucksvollen Burgruine Wertheim, dem Wahrzeichen der Stadt. Mit dem Bau der Burg wurde bereits Anfang des 12. Jahrhunderts begonnen, im Laufe der Jahrhunderte kam es immer wieder zu Erweiterungen. Kaiserliche Truppen zerstörten sie 1634. Wer sich für schöne mittelalterliche Schnitzwerke interessiert, der muss in Creglingen die Herrgottskirche (seit 1530 evangelisch) besuchen. Dort befindet sich der frei stehende Marienaltar des genialen Bildschnitzers Tilman Riemenschneider (um 1460–1531). Der um 1502–1505 geschnitzte Flügelaltar ist sieben Meter hoch und geöffnet etwa 3,5 Meter breit und gilt als das Hauptwerk der unterfränkischen Schule.

The picturesque old Frankish town of Wertheim, described by some people as "Little Heidelberg", lies at the confluence of the Tauber and Main. Among the town's many charming timbered houses, the house of the Ritter von Zobel (1520) on the market place is especially interesting. It is so narrow that the inhabitants could only put in their beds lengthways. On the ground floor you will find today a little shop selling glass ornaments. Passing the collegiate church and the late Gothic St. Kilian's Chapel, a stairway leads up to the magnificent ruined castle which is the landmark of Wertheim. The building of the castle began during the early twelfth century; over the centuries it was extended repeatedly. The Emperor's troops destroyed it in 1634. If you are interested in exquisite medieval carving you should visit the Herrgottskirche in Creglingen (Protestant since 1530). There you will find the free-standing Altar of the Virgin by the genial carver Tilman Riemenschneider (c. 1460-1531). The winged altar, carved in 1502-1505, is seven meters (23 feet) tall and some 3.5 meters (11 feet) wide when open. It is considered to be the supreme masterpiece of the Lower Franconian School.

Der Stammsitz der Herren von Hohenlohe befindet sich in Weikersheim. Das Schloss mit dem Park zählt zu den bedeutendsten Anlagen Baden-Württembergs. Ursprünglich als Wasserschloss angelegt – der staufische Bergfried ist aus dieser Zeit –, wurde es Ende des 16. Jahrhunderts im Renaissancestil ausgebaut. Zentraler Raum ist der Rittersaal. Der Park ist nach dem

Vorbild von Versailles als Barockgarten angelegt. Etwa 50 Kilometer weiter südlich befindet sich die Salzstadt Schwäbisch Hall, deren Solequelle bereits im 3. Jahrhundert v. Chr. keltische Siedler anlockte. Die malerische historische Altstadt mit ihren Renaissancehäusern lohnt einen Besuch. Am Marktplatz ist neben dem großen Brunnen der alte Pranger (frühes 16. Jahrhundert) zu sehen. Mit dem an einer Säule befestigten Halseisen wurden Verurteilte angekettet und so dem Spott der Passanten ausgesetzt – die Strafe bestand in der öffentlichen Schande. Bekannt ist Schwäbisch Hall heute auch durch die Freilichtspiele auf der großen Freitreppe vor der evangelischen Pfarrkirche St. Michael, dem Wahrzeichen der Stadt.

The main residence of the Lords of Hohenlohe is in Weikersheim. The castle and park are among the most important complexes in Baden-Württem-berg. Originally designed as a moated castle – the Hohenstaufen-era keep dates from this period –, it was extended in Renaissance style at the end of the 16th century. The Hall of Knights is the main room. The park is laid out as a Baroque garden in the style of Versailles. Some 50 kilometers (31 miles) further south is the salt-mining town of Schwäbisch Hall, whose brine spring attracted Celtic settlers as early as the third century B.C. The picturesque old city center with its Renaissance houses is worth a visit. On the market place, beside the big fountain, you can see the old pillory (early 16th century). Condemned criminals were chained to a pillar with an iron collar and were thus subjected to the mockery of passers-by: the punishment consisted of the public shame. Today Schwäbisch Hall is famous for its open-air plays on the steps in front of the Protestant Parish Church of St. Michael, the town's landmark sight.

Die Salzstadt Schwäbisch Hall liegt zu beiden Seiten des Flusses Kocher, einem der östlichen, rechtsseitigen Nebenflüsse des Neckar.

The salt-mining town of Schwäbisch Hall lies on both banks of the River Kocher, one of the eastern tributaries which joins the Neckar on the right bank.

Die schönsten Touren

The most picturesque tours

Die Autotour reiht wie an einer Perlenschnur die bekanntesten Orte Baden-Württembergs aneinander – ein idealer Mix aus reizvollen Landschaften, malerischen Städten sowie geschichtsträchtigen Schlössern und Burgen. Die beiden Radtouren führen durch eine ausgesucht schöne Landschaft, sie sind gut ausgeschildert und bieten begleitenden Service (Radausleihe, Gepäcktransport). Die genannten Wanderwege sind qualitätsgeprüft, leicht bis mittelschwer. Lange Touren können natürlich stets in Abschnitte (Tagestouren) unterteilt werden.

The driving tour links together the most famous places in Baden-Württemberg like a pearl necklace – an ideal blend of scenic beauty, picturesque towns and historic palaces and castles. The two cycling tours lead through the idyllic beauty of carefully selected countryside; they are well-signposted and offer an accompanying service (cycle hire, transportation of luggage). The hiking routes have been carefully checked and are easy to moderately demanding. Long tours can always be divided into sections (day trips).

„Die Fantastische Straße"

Heidelberg – Stuttgart – Calw – Tübingen – (Baden-Baden) – Burg Hohenzollern – Meersburg – Konstanz, 400 km

Die „Fantastische Straße" ist eine touristische Route, die dem Reisenden einige der attraktivesten Städte Baden-Württembergs näher bringen soll. Vom romantischen Heidelberg im Norden bis zum Bodensee im Süden befinden sich neun der schönsten Städte des Landes auf dieser Strecke. Der Weg führt in Altstädte mit ihren gepflegten Fachwerkhäusern, durch die herrliche Landschaft des Schwarzwalds und der Schwäbischen Alb, vorbei an Burgen und Schlössern wie der Stammburg des letzten deutschen Kaisers. Die Fahrt sollte auf mehrere Tage verteilt werden.

The "Fantastic Road" is a tourist route which aims to show the traveler some of the most picturesque towns in Baden-Württemberg. From Romantic Heidelberg in the north to Lake Constance in the south, nine of the most attractive towns in the region lie along this route. It leads into old towns with immaculate timbered houses, through the magnificent landscape of the Black Forest and the Swabian Alb, past castles and palaces including the residence of the last German emperor. The journey should be divided into several days.

Info: www.fantastische-strasse.de

Bodensee-Radweg

Konstanz – Bregenz – Romanshorn, 270 km

Der Bodensee-Radweg ist eine der beliebtesten europäischen Radrouten. Bis spätestens 16 Uhr anrufen und ein Service holt am folgenden Morgen den Koffer ab und transportiert ihn für eine Handvoll Euro zur Zielherberge (die frei wählbar ist).

The Lake Constance Cycle Path is one of the most popular cycle routes in Europe. If you phone before 4 p.m. your suitcase will be collected the next morning and transported for a few euros to the inn which is your destination for that day (which can be chosen freely).

Info: www.bodensee-radweg.com

Neckartalradweg

Schwenningen – Rottenburg – Bad Cannstatt – Bad Wimpfen – Heidelberg – Mannheim, 370 km

Vier Tage sollte veranschlagen, wer den gesamten Weg zurücklegen möchte. Natürlich kann man auch einzelne Etappen wählen. Einige Streckenabschnitte, vor allem über die Schwäbische Alb, sind etwas anspruchsvoller.

If you want to cycle along the entire route you should allow four days. Of course you can also just cycle along individual stretches; you will never be disappointed. Some sections, especially that leading through the Swabian Alp, are more energetic.

Info: www.neckarradweg.de

*Fünf Genießertouren – mit dem Auto (rot), mit dem Fahrrad (grün)
und zu Fuß (violett).*

*Five of the most beautiful tours –
by car (red), with the bicycle (green) or on foot (purple).*

Baiersbronner Seensteig

*Start: Bahnhof Baiersbronn, 84 km
(3-4 Tage/3-4 days)*

Der Seensteig zu den Karseen und den höchsten Bergen des Nordschwarzwalds ist einer der Top-Wanderwege Deutschlands. Der Rundkurs beginnt am Wander-Informationszentrum am Bahnhof Baiersbronn.

The lake climb to the cirque lakes and the highest mountains of the north Black Forest is one of the top hiking routes in Germany. The circuit starts by the hikers' information center at Baiersbronn railroad station.

Info: www.baiersbronn.de

Donauberglandweg

*Lemberg – Wehingen – Mühlheim a.d.Donau – Kloster Beuron, 60 km
(3 Tage/3 days)*

Von den höchsten Bergen der Schwäbischen Alb führt der Weg in die wildromantische Weißjura-Felsenwelt des Donaudurchbruchstals im Herzen des Naturparks Obere Donau. Gut 4000 Höhenmeter an Steigungen und Abstiegen gilt es bis zum Ziel, die Benediktiner-Erzabtei Beuron, zu überwinden.

The route leads from the highest mountains of the Swabian Alb into the wildromantic rocky world of the white Jurassic limestone which characterizes the Danube valley in the heart of the Upper Danube nature park. You will have to cope with over 4000 meters (13,120 feet) of ascents and descents before you reach Beuron.

Info: www.donaubergland.de

Ereignisse und Feste im Jahreskreis

Events and celebrations around the year

Frühling (Spring)

Fastnacht / „Fasnet" (Carnival)

Sobald mit dem Dreikönigstag am 6. Januar die weihnachtlichen Feiertage ihr Ende finden, beginnt in Baden-Württemberg die Zeit der Fastnacht, in schwäbischer Mundart die „Fasnet".

As soon as the Christmas festivities draw to an end at Epiphany (January 6), Baden-Württemberg begins its carnival celebrations (Fastnacht), known in Swabian as "Fasnet".

- Donaueschingen
- Elzach (Schuddig-Umzug)
- Oberndorf
- Rottweil (Narrensprung)
- Überlingen
- Villingen-Schwenningen

Heilbronner Pferdemarkt (Heilbronn Horse Fair)

Jedes Jahr am letzten Februarwochenende findet in Heilbronn ein bunt-turbulentes Treiben mit Händlern, Imbissbuden und Fahrgeschäften statt.

Every year on the last weekend in February, Heilbronn is transformed into a colorful, lively fair with goods for sale, snack stalls and rides.

Maimarkt Mannheim (Mannheim May Fair)

Höhepunkt des Mannheimer Maimarkts (elf Tage ab dem letzten Aprilsamstag) ist ein Reitturnier.

The highlight of the Mannheim May Fair (eleven days following the last Saturday in April) is a riding tournament.

Kuchen- und Brunnenfest der Salzsieder in Schwäbisch Hall (Pfingsten) (Salters' Festival) (Whitsun)

Das Salzsiederfest Ende Mai feiern die Schwäbisch-Haller schon seit dem 14. Jahrhundert.

The citizens of Schwäbisch Hall celebrate the Salters' Festival at the end of May since the 14th century.

Nebelhöhlenfest (Pfingsten) (Cave Festival) (Whitsun)

In Sonnenbühl wird diese Fest seit 1803 jedes Jahr zu Pfingsten gefeiert. Namensgebend ist die Nebelhöhle, eine Tropfsteinhöhle von insgesamt 803 Metern Länge (für Besucher zugänglich).

The festival has been celebrated in Sonnenbühl every year at Whitsun since 1803. It is named after the Nebelhöhle, a stalagmite cave which is a total of 803 meters (2634 feet) in length and which is open to visitors.

Tübinger Stocherkahnrennen (Tübingen Punt Race)

Kurz vor Sommeranfang (an einem Junidonnerstag) findet seit 1956 das Tübinger Stocherkahnrennen statt.

Since 1956 the Tübingen Punt Race has been held on a Thursday in June shortly before the beginning of summer.

Sommer (Summer)

Peter-und-Paul-Fest in Bretten (Anfang Juli) (Festival of St. Peter and St. Paul in Bretten)(Early July)

Am ersten Wochenende nach Peter und Paul (29. Juni) geht es vier Tage lang in Bretten auf dem größten Mittelalterfest Südwestdeutschlands hoch her.

The largest medieval festival in southwest Germany is celebrated with great gusto on the first weekend after the Festival of St. Peter and St. Paul in Bretten.

Ravensburger Rutenfest

Jedes Jahr gegen Ende Juli, kurz bevor in Baden-Württemberg die Sommerferien beginnen, feiert man in Ravensburg das Rutenfest.

The Rutenfest is celebrated in Ravensburg annually towards the end of July, before the school summer holidays begin in Baden-Württemberg.

Schwörmontag in Ulm

Eine ganz besondere Feierlichkeit ist der Schwörmontag in Ulm, der auf den vorletzten Montag im Juli fällt.

Schwörmontag, held in Ulm on the last Monday but one in July, is a very special celebration.

Konstanzer Seenachtsfest (Anfang August) (Konstanz Night Festival) (Beginning of August)

Das größte Volksfest am Bodensee: In der Nacht erstrahlt die spiegelglatte Wasserfläche im Licht eines spektakulären Höhenfeuerwerks, tagsüber spielen Livebands, auf der Hafenstraße ist ein Markt aufgebaut.

The largest folk festival on Lake Constance: The mirror-calm waters sparkle in the lights of a spectacular firework display. During the day live bands play and a market is held on the Hafenstrasse.

Stuttgarter Weindorf (Wine Festival)

Ende August bis Anfang September zieht es Weinkenner scharenweise nach Stuttgart zum Stuttgarter Weindorf.

At the end of August or beginning of September, wine experts flock to the Stuttgarter Weindorf in Stuttgart.

Weinfeste am Kaiserstuhl und Tuniberg (Wine festivals on the Kaiserstuhl and Tuniberg)

Diverse Feste zwischen Juli und September in Breisach und Vogtsburg.

Various festivals are held between July and September in Breisach and Vogtsburg.

HERBST (FALL)

Cannstatter Volksfest (Folk Festival)

Großes Volksfest auf dem Cannstatter Wasen, das eine Woche nach Ende des Oktoberfests beginnt. Eingeführt 1818 als landwirtschaftliches Fest.

A big folk festival is held on the Wasen in Cannstatt, beginning one week after the end of Munich's Oktoberfest. It was introduced in 1818 as an agricultural festival.

Fellbacher Herbst (Fall Festival)

Eines der größten Wein- und Erntedankfeste findet am zweiten Oktoberwo-chenende in Fellbach, einer Stadt wenige Kilometer östlich von Stuttgart, statt.

One of the largest wine and harvest festivals is held in Fellbach near Stuttgart on the second weekend in October.

WINTER (WINTER)

Ludwigsburger Weihnachtsmarkt (Ludwigsburg Christmas Market)

Zu den absoluten Highlights unter den baden-württembergischen Weihnachtsmärkten zählt der Barock-Weihnachtsmarkt in Ludwigsburg.

The Baroque Christmas market in Ludwigsburg is one of the absolute highlights among the Christmas markets of Baden-Württemberg.

Weihnachtsmarkt in Bad Wimpfen (Christmas Market in Bad Wimpfen)

Das vorweihnachtliche Marktgeschehen entwickelte sich aus dem Katharinenmarkt (erstmals 1487).

The pre-Christmas market developed from the Katharinenmarkt (first held in 1487).

Weihnachtsmarkt Gengenbach (Christmas Market in Gengenbach)

Das größte Adventskalenderhaus der Welt befindet sich in Gegenbach: In der Vorweihnachtszeit blickt den Besuchern des Weihnachtsmarkts aus den 24 Fenstern des klassizistischen Rathauses jeden Tag ein weiteres Bild eines berühmten Künstlers entgegen.

The largest Advent Calendar in the world in the form of a house: In the 24 windows of the neo-Classical Town Hall, visitors to the Christmas market can see another painting by a famous artist every day during the pre-Christmas season.

Weihnachtsmarkt Ulm (Ulm Christmas Market)

Im Hintergrund das imposante Ulmer Münster, vor sich mehr als 100 weihnachtlich aufgeputzte Stände.

The imposing cathedral of Ulm serves as backdrop for more than 100 seasonally decorated Christmas stands.

Stuttgarter Weihnachtsmarkt (Stuttgart Christmas Market)

Einer der größten Weihnachtsmärkte Europas. Vor der Kulisse des Stuttgarter Schlosses breitet sich ein wahres Weihnachtsland aus und im Schlosshof begeistert das märchenhafte Kinderland nicht nur kleine Besucher.

One of the largest Christmas markets in Europe. A Christmas paradise extends with the Stuttgarter Schloss in the background. The fairy-tale children's wonderland in the palace courtyards delights not only young visitors.

Register | *Index*

Verweise auf Abbildungen sind kursiv | *References to pictures are in italics*

Bildnachweis | Credits

Umschlag-Vorderseite:
Titelbild, Heidelberg, Neckarbrücke und Schloss: TopicMedia/KKK
Kleine Bilder, von links nach rechts: Stuttgart neues Schloss: TopicMedia/MWI; Freiburg, Blaue Brücke und Herz.Jesu-Kirche: TopicMedia/MKF; Schwarzwaldmädel: TopicMedia/OTT; Hölderlinturm und Neckar, Tübingen: Jörg Launer-Fotolia.com
Umschlag-Rückseite:
Hohenzollernschloss Sigmaringen: TopicMedia/MKF; Neue Staatgalerie, Stuttgart: TopicMedia/MWI; Weinberge im Schwarzwald: reises-Fotolia.com; Schillergeburtshaus, Marbach: TopicMedia/MWI; Luftbild Reichenau: Gerhard Launer-Luftbild
Seite 1: TopicMedia/JBE; 2: mauritius images/Uta und Horst Kolley; 4, 5: TopicMedia/MKF; 8: Stihl024/Pixelio; 9: mauritius images/imagebroker/Silwen Randebrock; 11: reises-Fotolia.com; 12, 13: TopicMedia/MWI; TopicMedia/SCE; TopicMedia/IMW; TopicMedia/OTT; TopicMedia/HAM; 14, 15: TopicMedia/MWI; TopicMedia/BEL; TopicMedia/OTT; TopicMedia/MWI; 17: Gerhard Launer-Luftbild; 19: picture alliance/Paul Mayall; 20: TopicMedia/MWI; 21 o. von li.: going-klick/shotshop.com; martine wagner-Fotolia.com; TopicMedia/MWI; 21 u.: gavioneta-Fotolia.com; 23 v. li.o.:TopicMedia/FEL; 23 re. o.:Ulrich Willmünder-Fotolia.com; 23 li. u.: Reinhard Pietsch; 23 re. u.: mauritius images/imagebroker/Michael Weber; 24: mauritius images/Hicazi Özdemir; 25: Michael S. Schwarzer-Fotolia.com; 26, 27 v. li.: TopicMedia/MKF (und Ausschnitt S.90); Reinhard Pietsch; TopicMedia/MKF; TopicMedia/WGA; Cazador-Fotolia.com; 29: Gerhard Launer-Luftbild; 30: TopicMedia/MKL; 31: TopicMedia/SIK; 33: i.reiser/pixelio; 34, 35: v. li.: mauritius images/Werner Otto; TopicMedia/SIR; TopicMedia/JBE; TopicMedia/OTT; 36: TopicMedia/MWI (2); 37: TopicMedia/KFS; ullstein bild; TopicMedia/SIR; 39: Jörg Launer-Fotolia.com; 40: Udo Kroener-Fotolia.com; 41: Gerhard Köhler-Fotolia.com; TopicMedia/MKF; TopicMedia/MKL; Gerhard Launer-Luftbild; 43 v. li. o.: TopicMedia/OTT; mauritius images/Karl-Heinz Hänel; mauritius images/Hicazi Özdemir; mauritius images/Robert Knöll; 45: TopicMedia/MKL; 47 v. li. o.: Georg Schlierling/shotshop.com; Gerhard Gebener/PIXELIO; Herbert Hartmann; TopicMedia/OTT; 48: TopicMedia/HAM; 49 o. v. li.: mauritius images/Robert Knöll; TopicMedia/KAS; TopicMedia/JBE; Bildagentur Huber/R. Schmid; 51 v. li. o.: Gerhard Launer-Luftbild; Sonja-Fotolia.com; terranova_17-Fotolia.com; TopicMedia/OTT; 52: mauritius images/Peter Widmann; 53: TopicMedia/FGL; 54: Alldale/shotshop.com; 55: Willi Wilhelm-Fotolia.com; TopicMedia/MKF; www.jenshagen.info-Fotolia.com; 57: Klaus Eppele-Fotolia.com; 58: Herbert Hartmann; 59: reises-Fotolia.com; 60: Gerhard Launer-Luftbild; 61: TopicMedia/MWI; TopicMedia/BAH (2); TopicMedia/KAS; 62: TopicMedia/CHF; 63: Daniel Kocherscheidt/shotshop.com; 65:TopicMedia/BAH; 66: Gerhard Launer-Luftbild; 67: TopicMedia/LUH; 68: Reises-Fotolia.com; 69: mauritius images/imagebroker/Helmut Meyer zur Capellen; 70: Herbert Hartmann; 71: Volker Rauch/shotshop.com; Herbert Hartmann; mauritius images/Uta und Horst Kolley; Herbert Hartmann; 73: mauritius images/Fritz Mader; mauritius images/Manfred Mehlig; 74: Roswitha Keller-Fotolia.com; 75: TopicMedia/MMX; 77:TopicMedia/DBN; 78: mauritius images/Robert Knöll; Herbert Hartmann; 81 v. li. o.: TopicMedia/PAW; TopicMedia/SIR (2); mauritius images/imagebroker/BAO; 82: Herbert Hartmann; 83: mauritius images/Robert Knöll; 85 v. li. o.: TopicMedia/SZM; TopicMedia/OTT; Wolfgang Wehl/PIXELIO; TopicMedia/SZM; 86: mauritius images/Robert Knöll; Mi Gr/Shotshop.com; 89: Herbert Hartmann; 92: Michael Fritzen-Fotolia.com; 93: TopicMedia/MWI.

Bibliografische Information Der Deutschen Nationalbibliothek
Die Deutsche Nationalbibliothek verzeichnet diese Publikation in der Deutschen Nationalbibliografie; detaillierte bibliografische Daten sind im Internet unter http://dnb.d-nb.de abrufbar.

Deutsche Originalausgabe
Copyright © 2009 von dem Knesebeck GmbH & Co. Verlags KG, München
Ein Unternehmen der La Martinière Groupe

Text und Konzeption: Dr. Reinhard Pietsch
Redaktion: Cornelia Schmidt
Gestaltung und Satz: Christine Paxmann text • konzept • grafik
Kartographie: Heidi Schmalfuß, München
Lithografie: Repro-Ludwig, A-Zell am See
Druck und Bindung: Mohn Media, Gütersloh
Printed in Germany

ISBN 978-3-86873-024-1

www.knesebeck-verlag.de